Petopia - A Photobook

A Whimsical Showcase of Adorable Companions

By Photopydia

"I am fond of pigs. Dogs look up to us. Cats lookdown on us. Pigs treat us as equals." - Winston Churchill

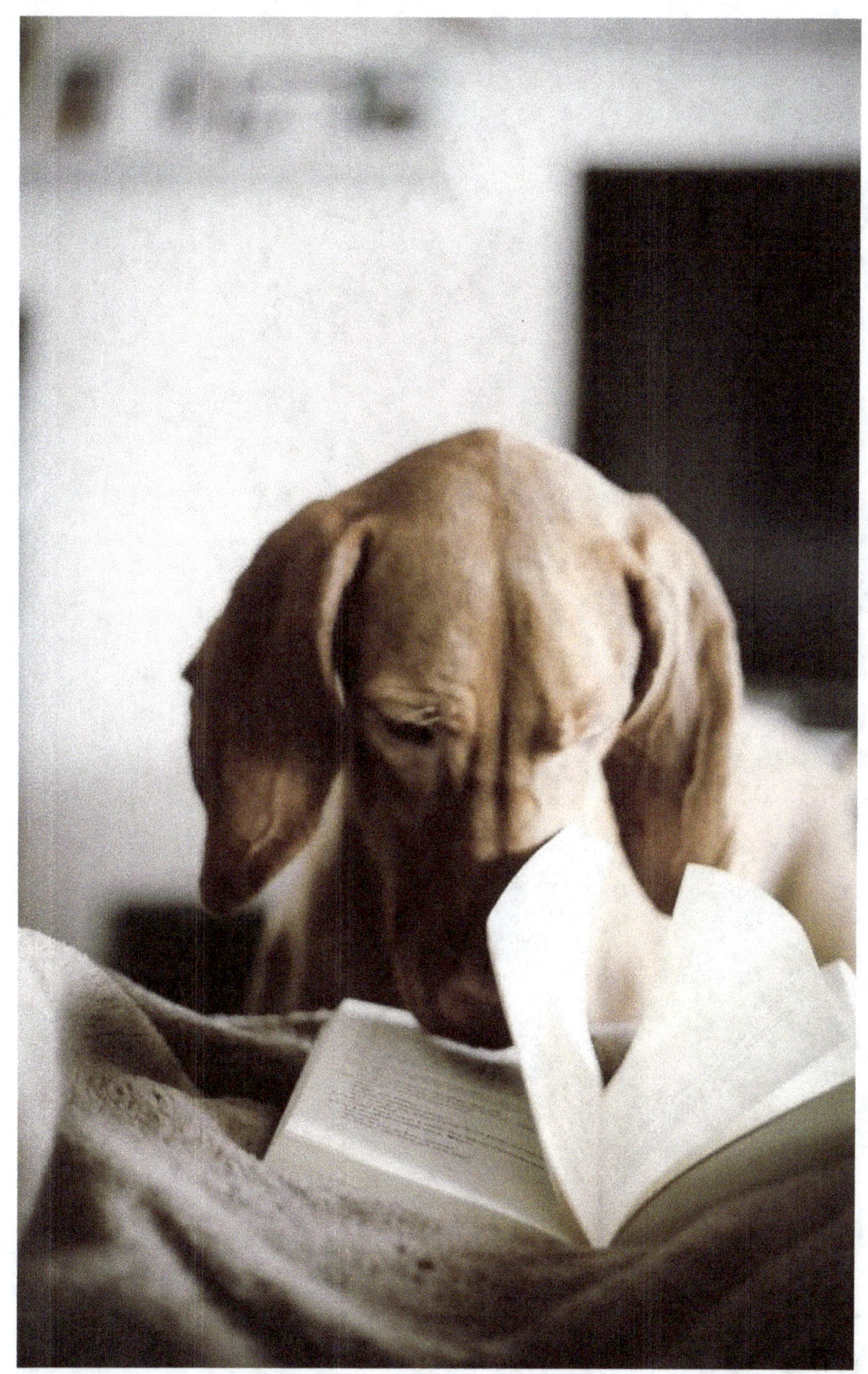

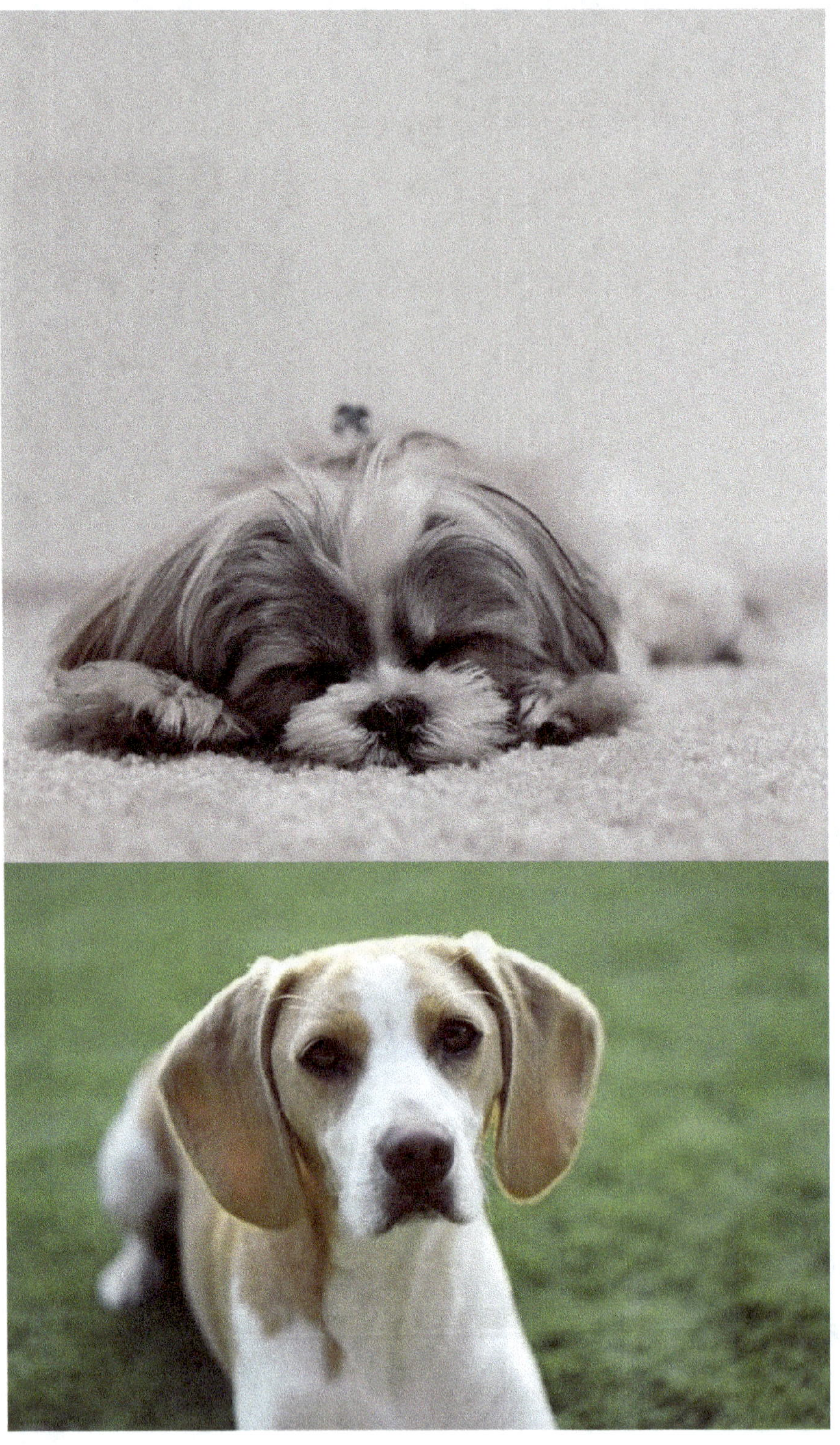

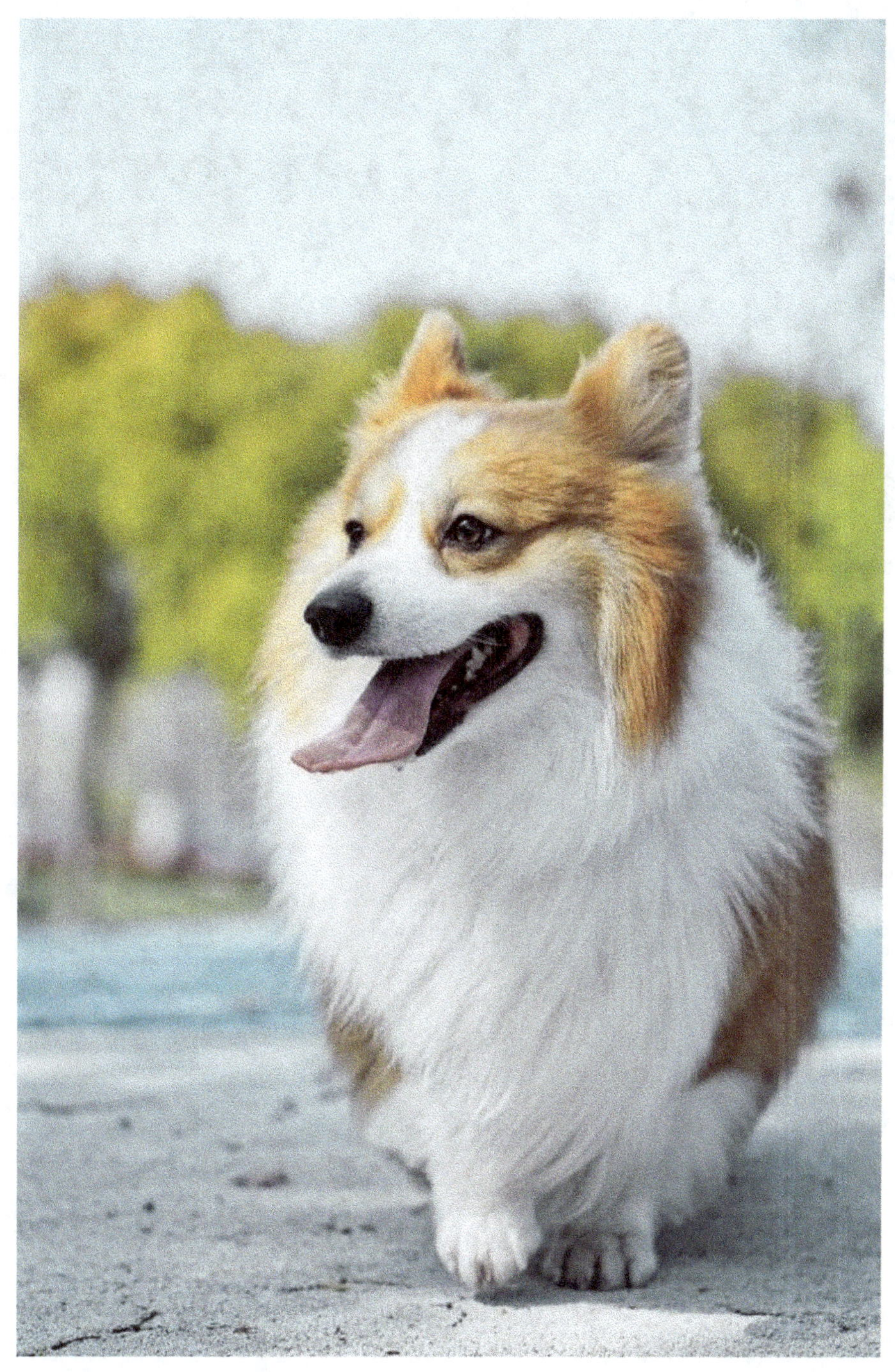

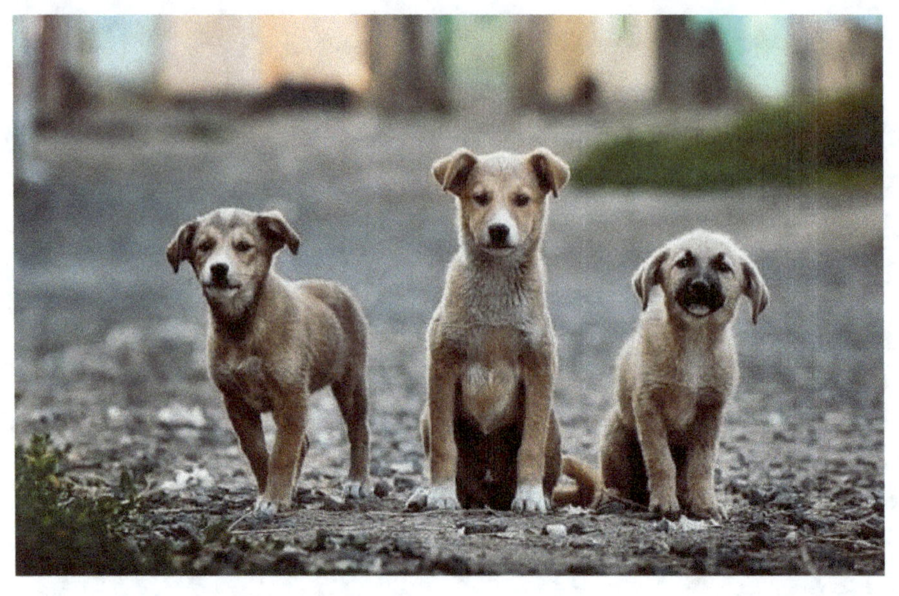

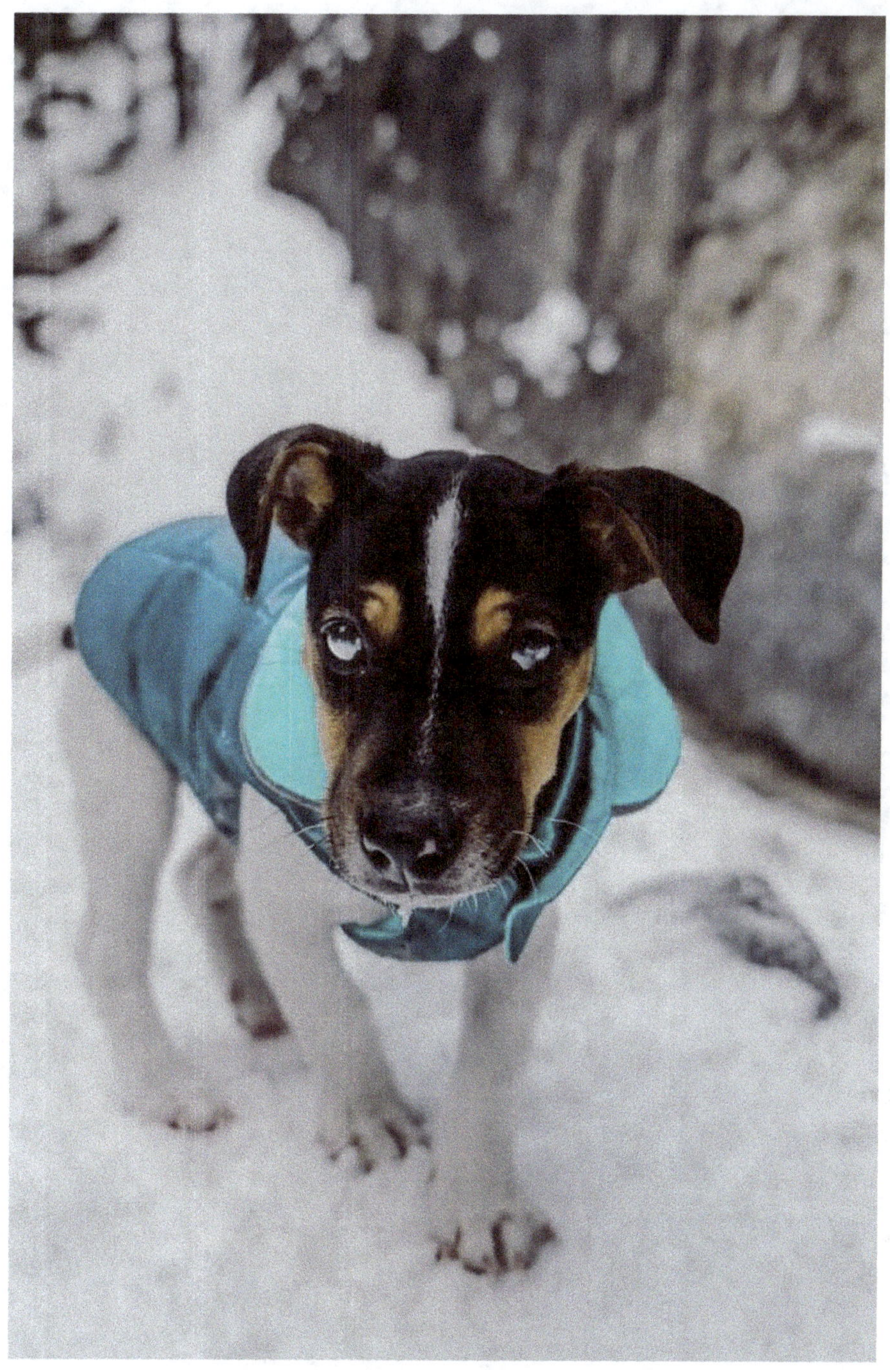

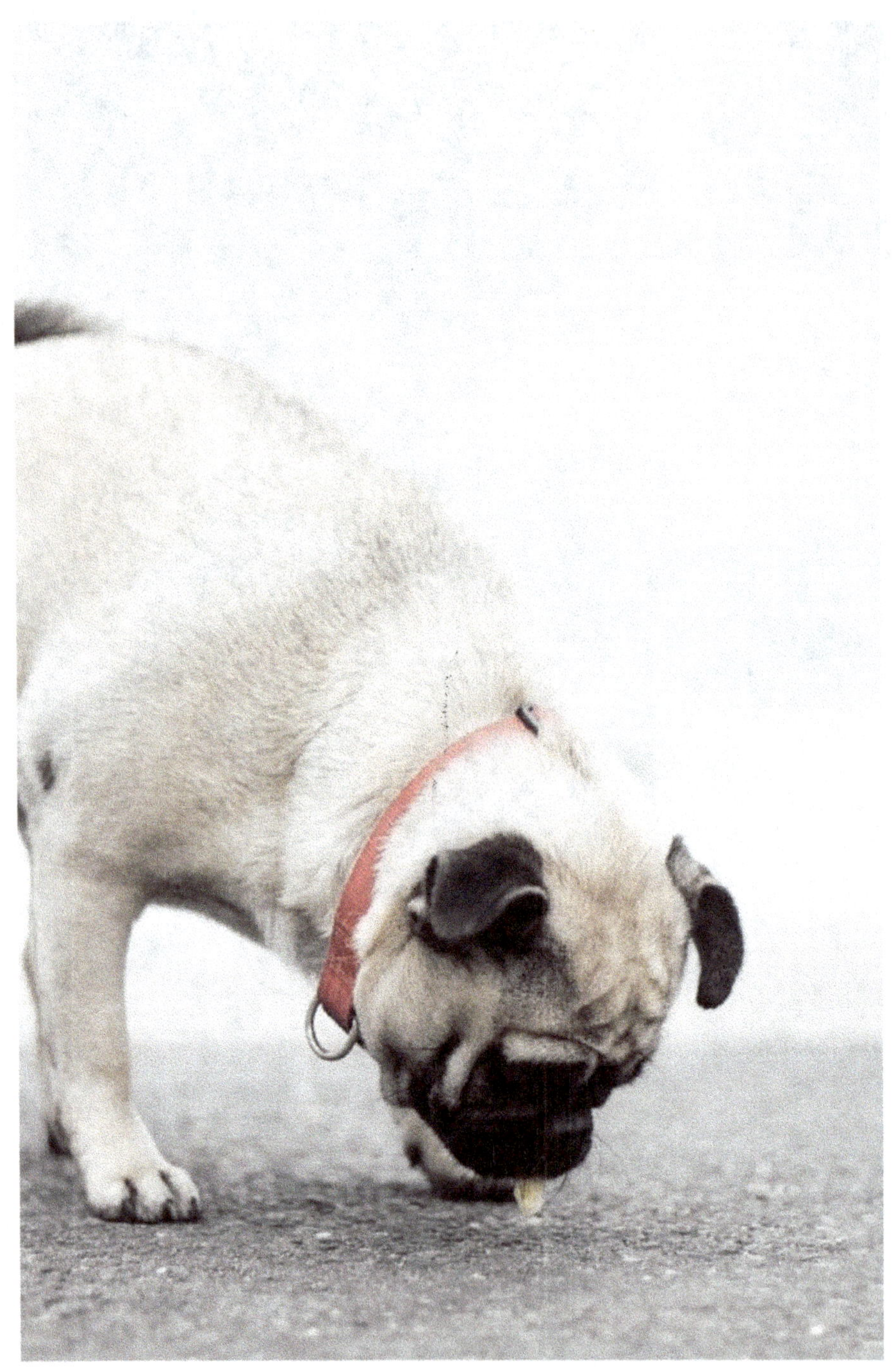

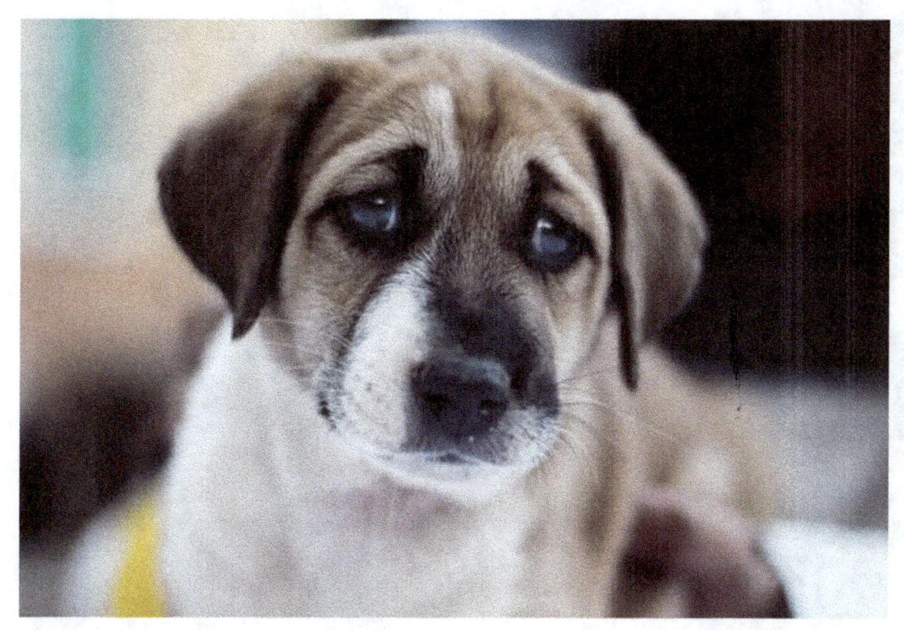

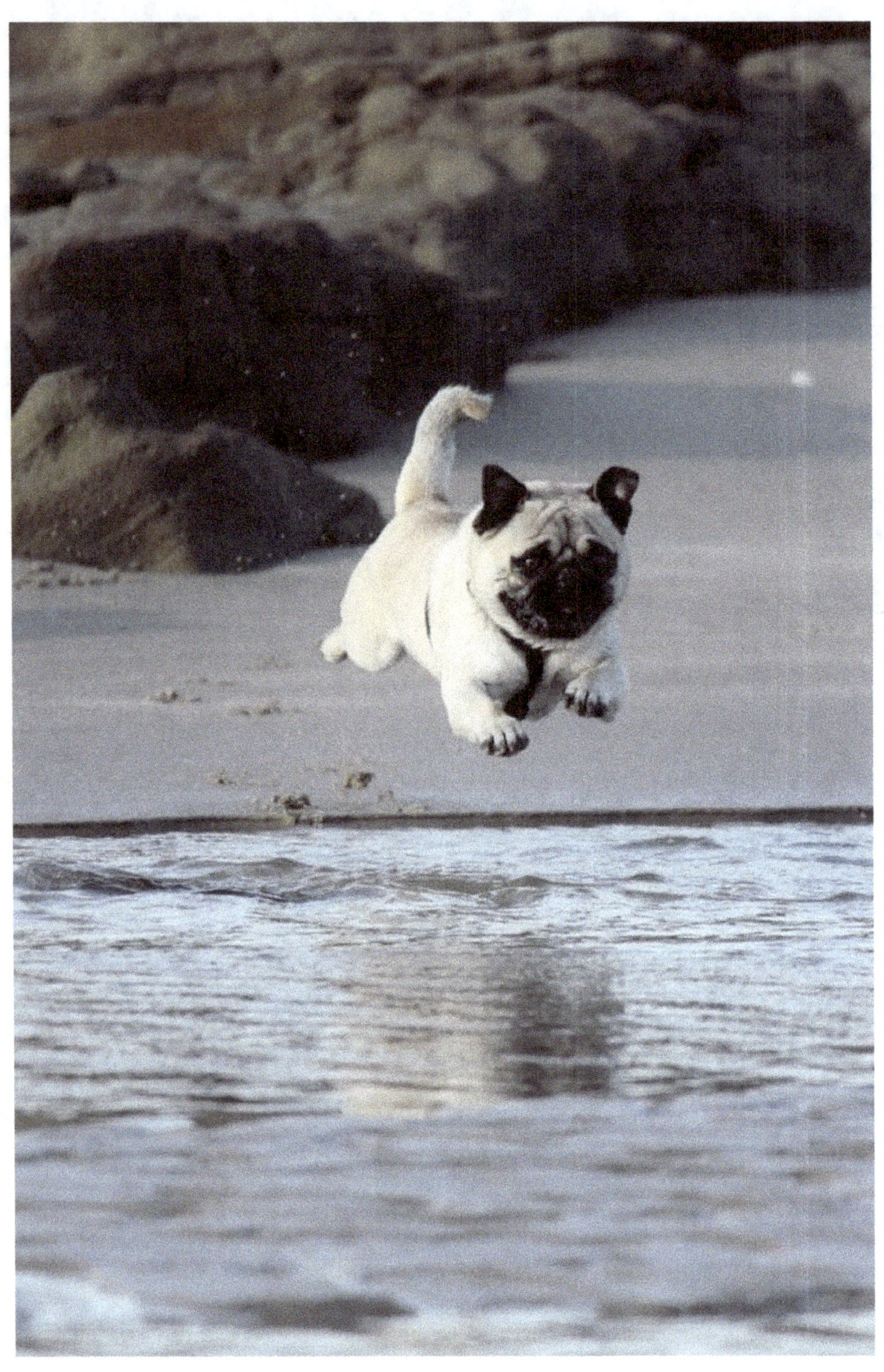

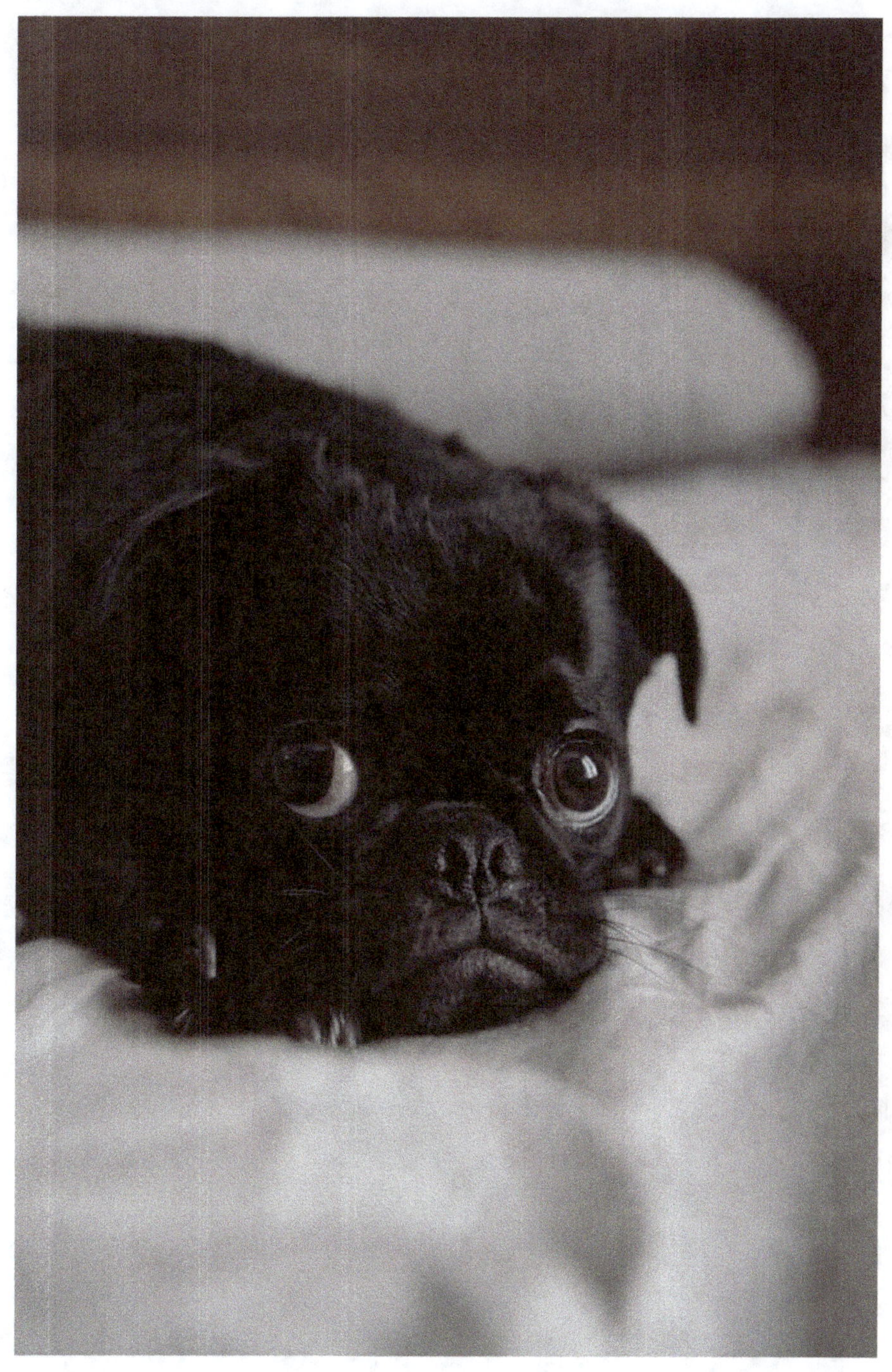

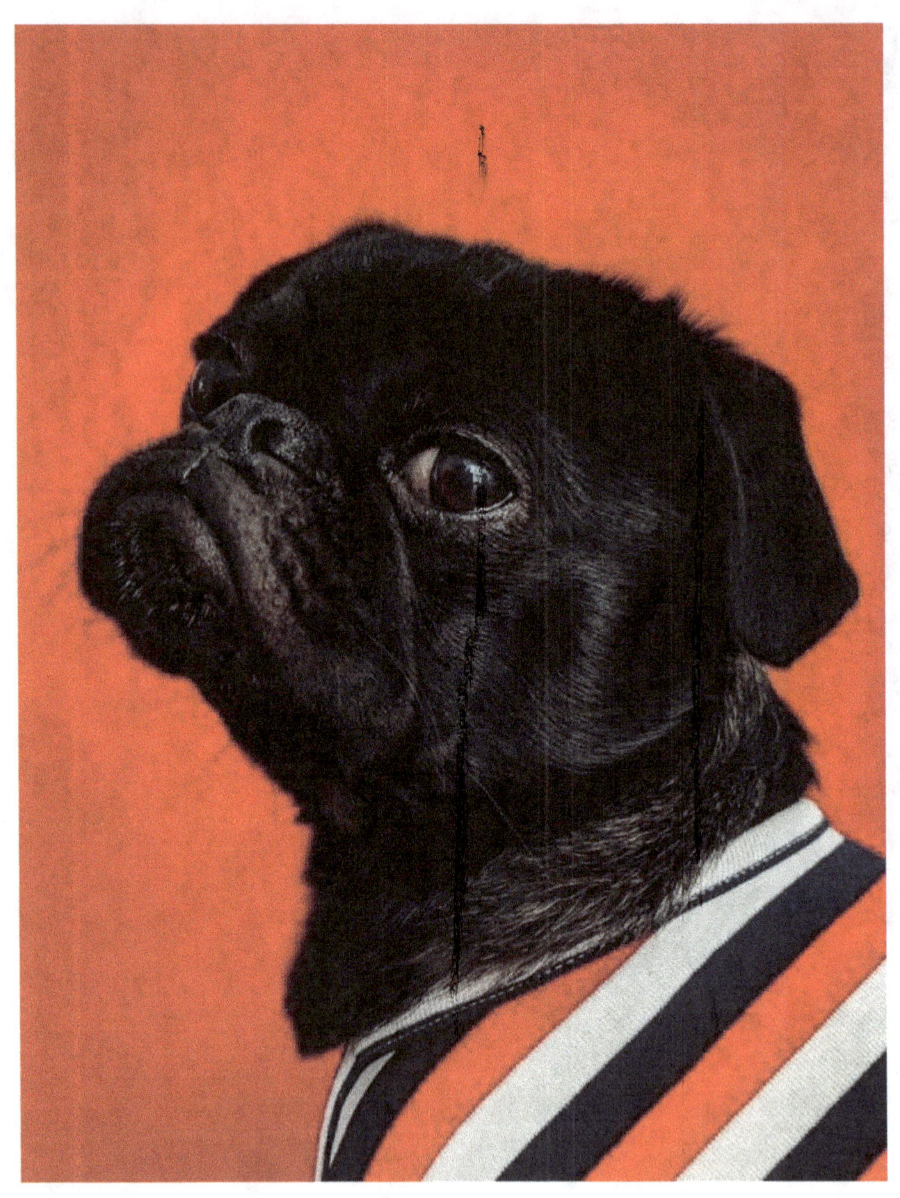

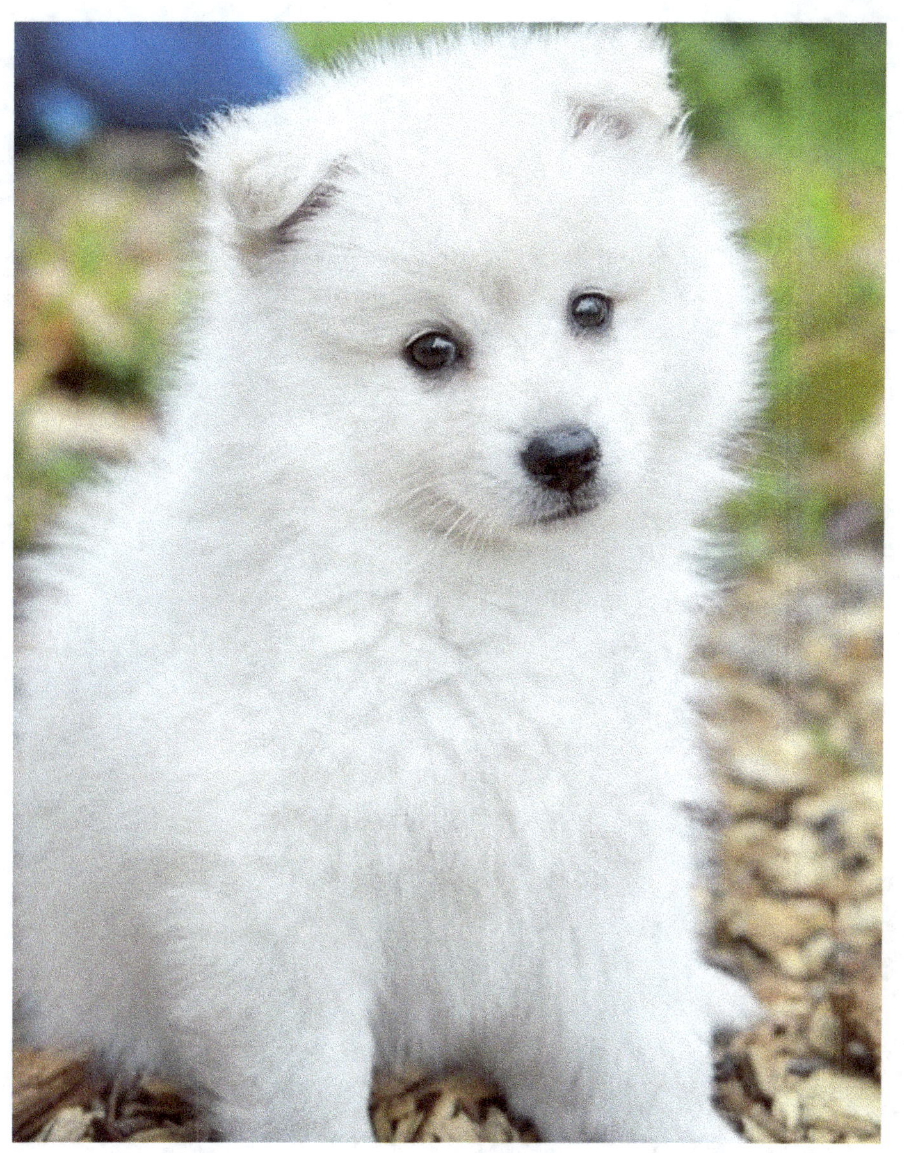

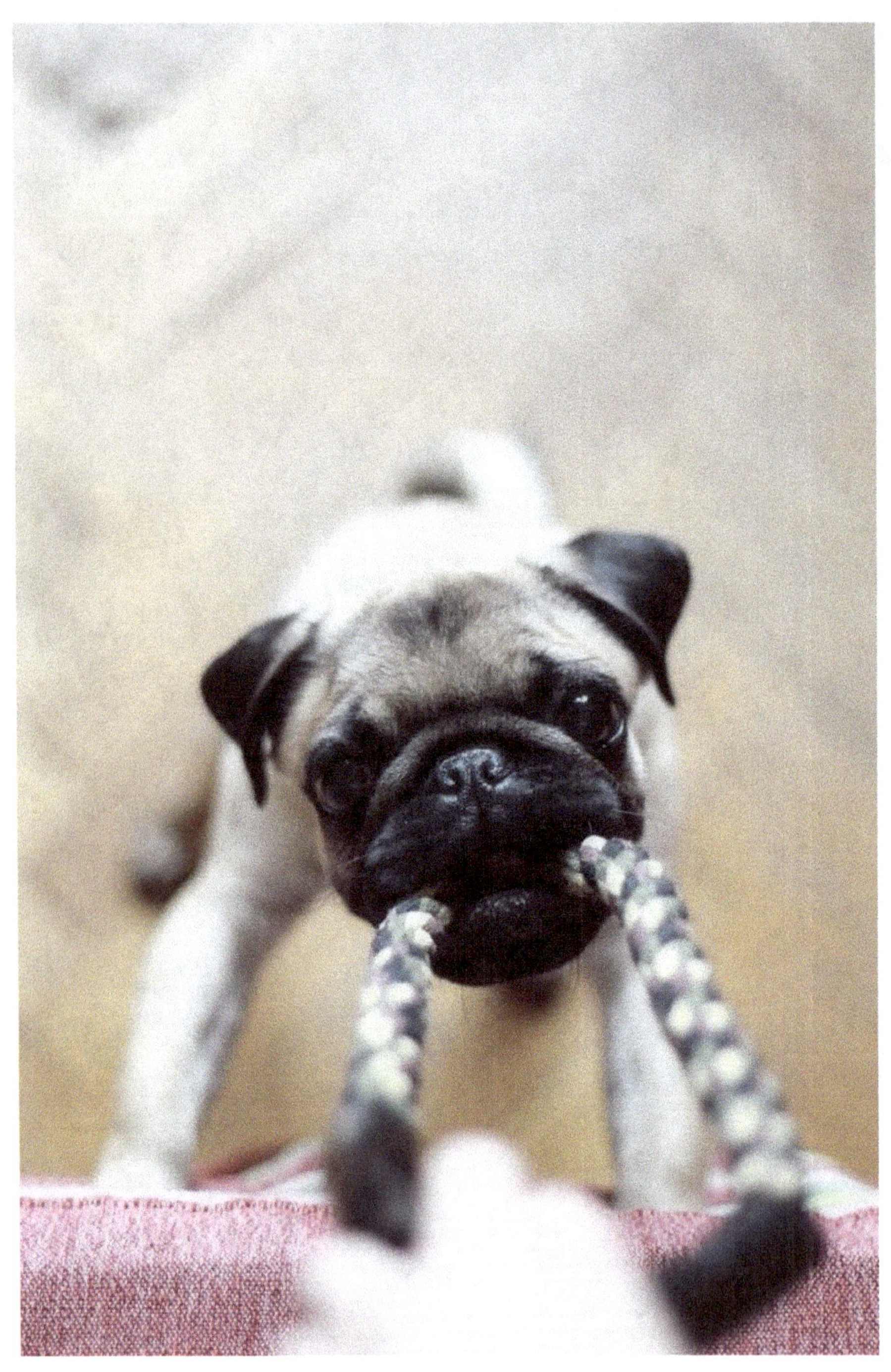

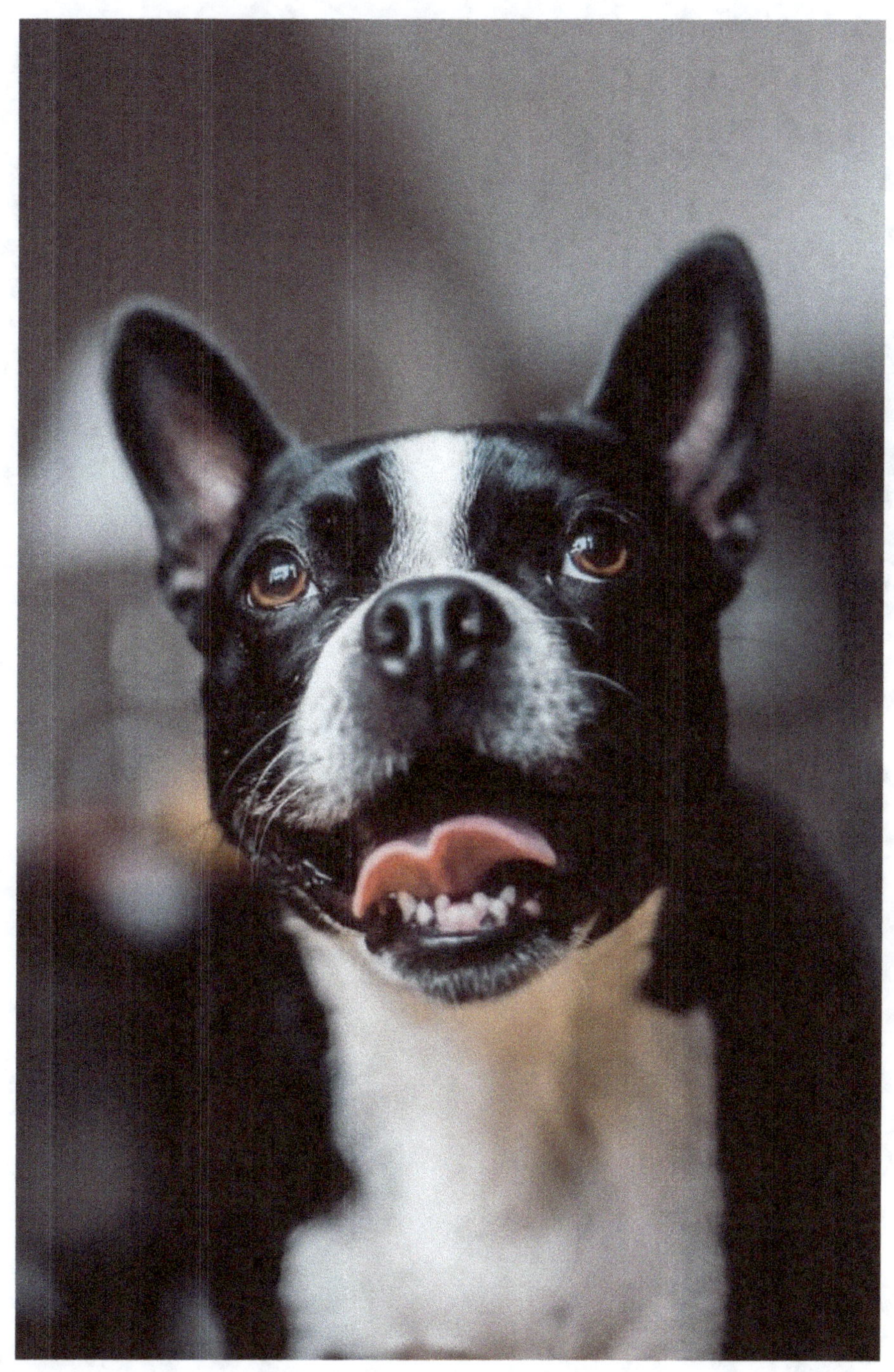

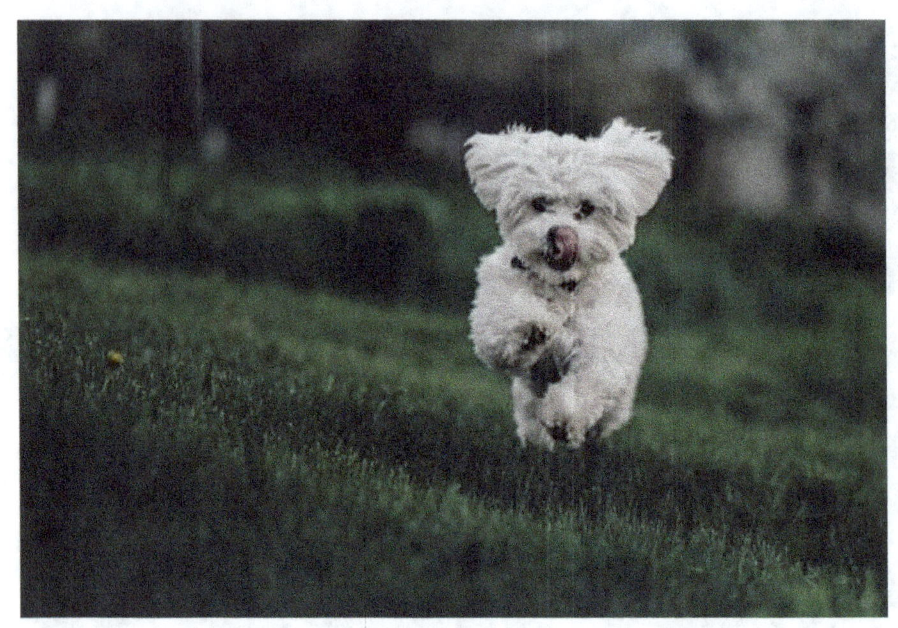

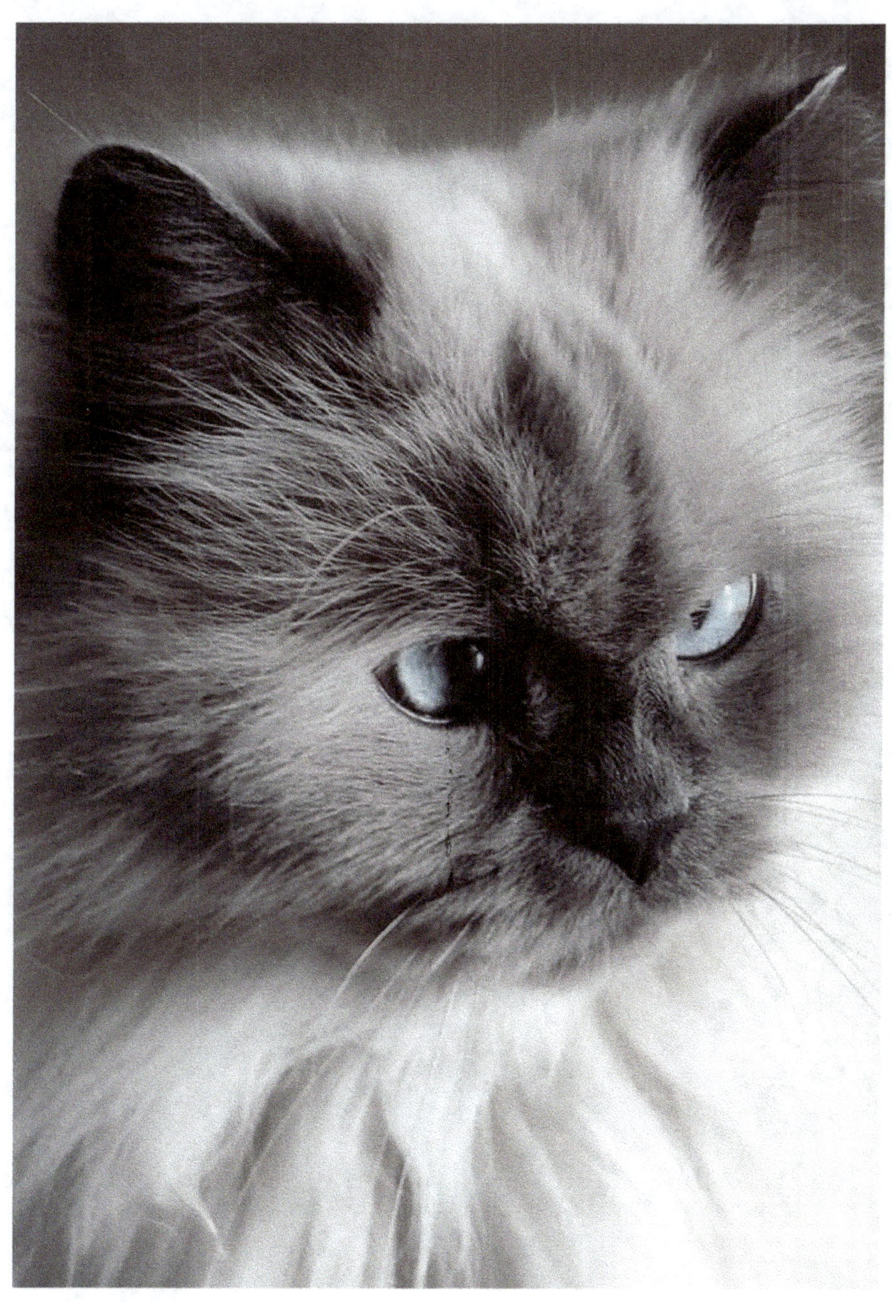

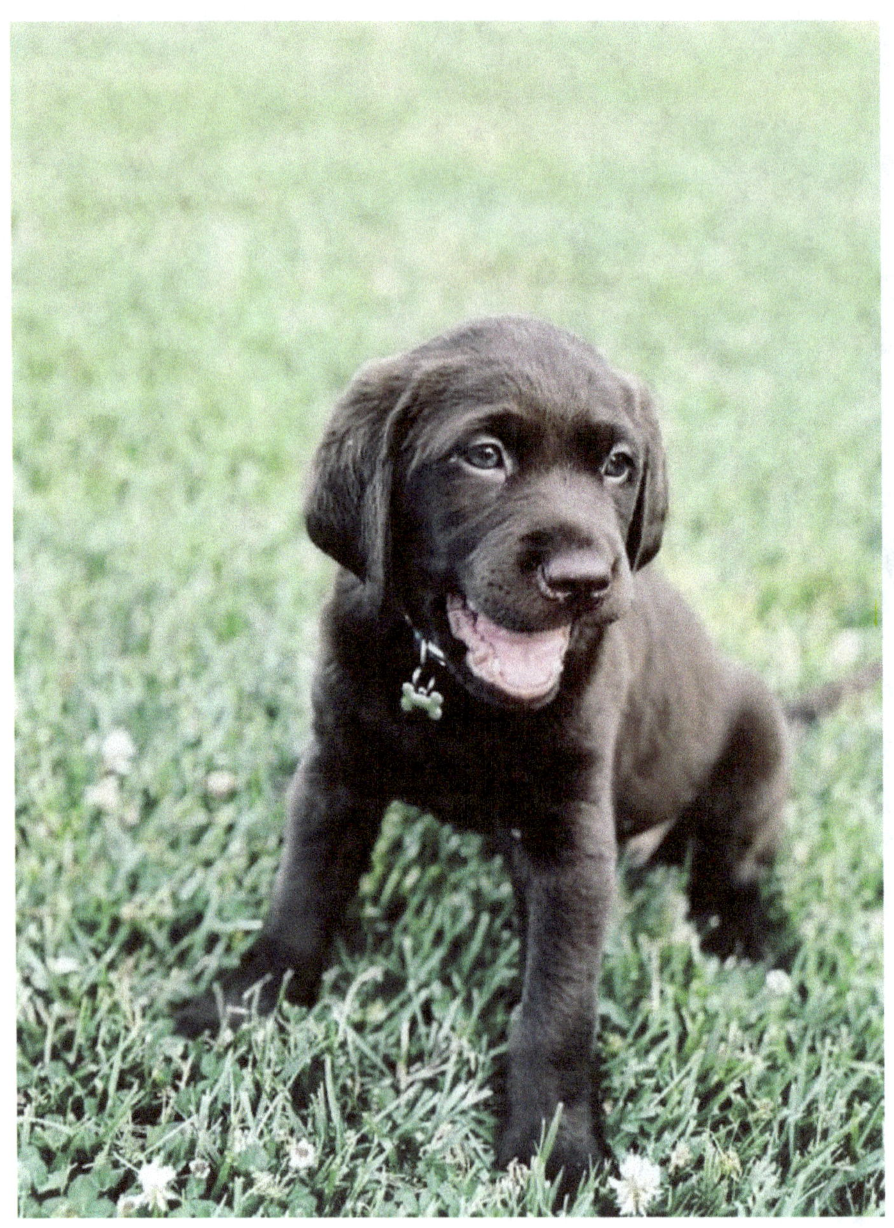

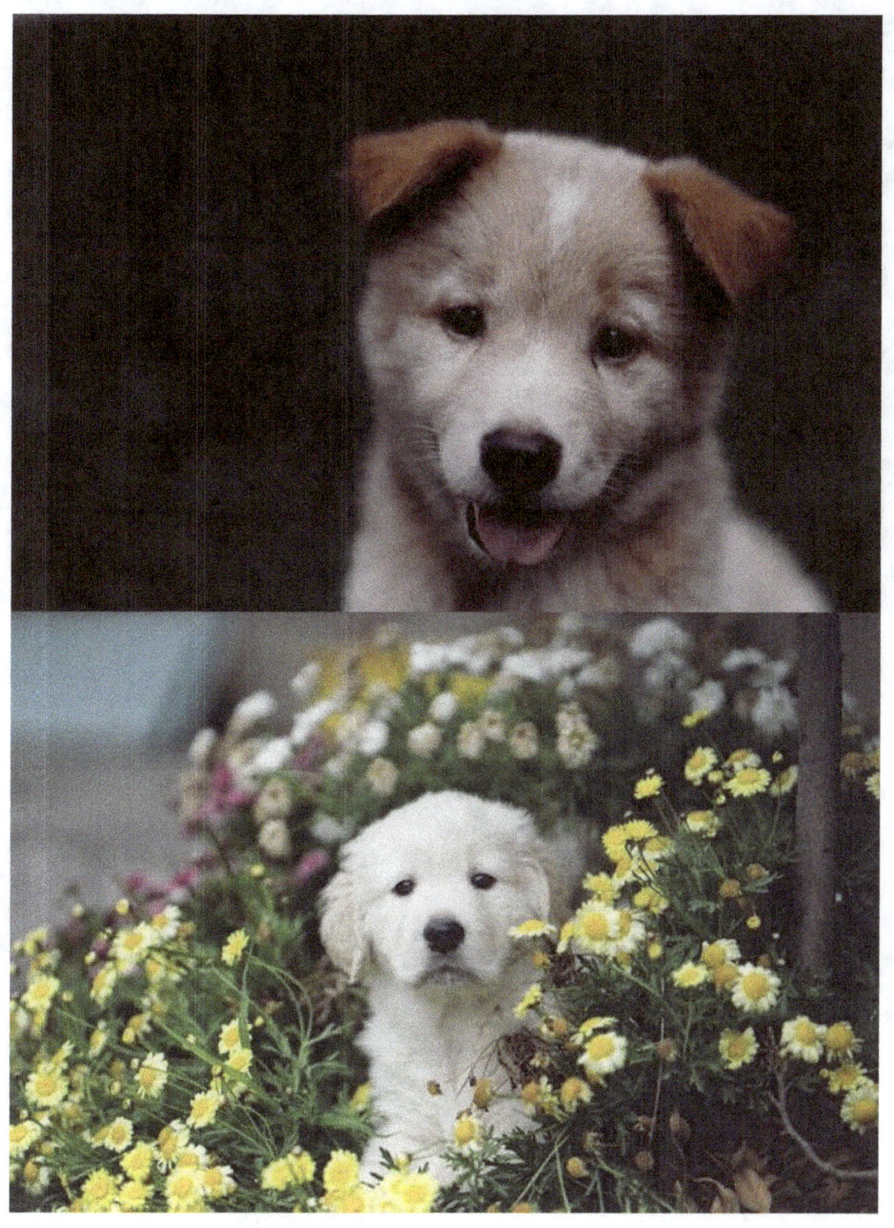

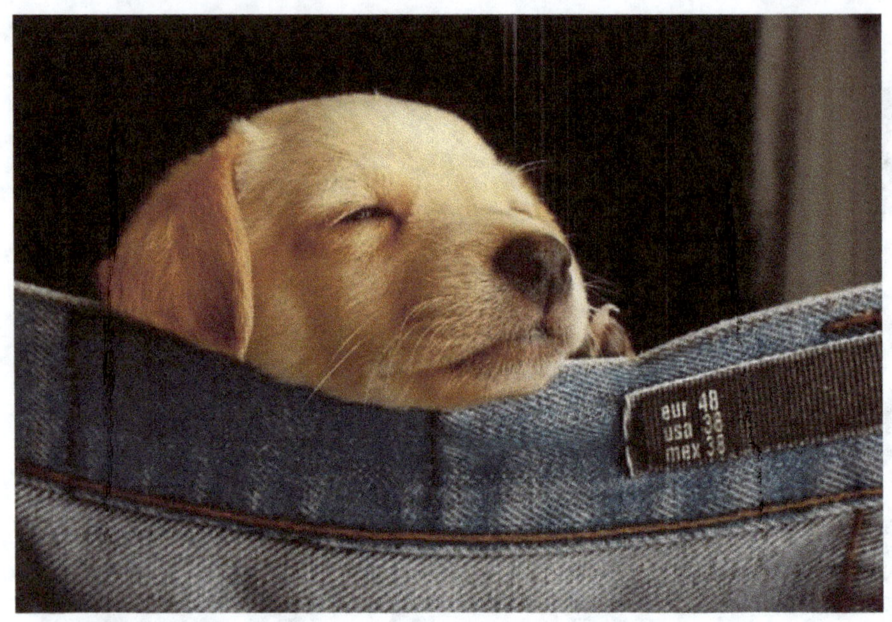

eur 48
usa 38
mex 38

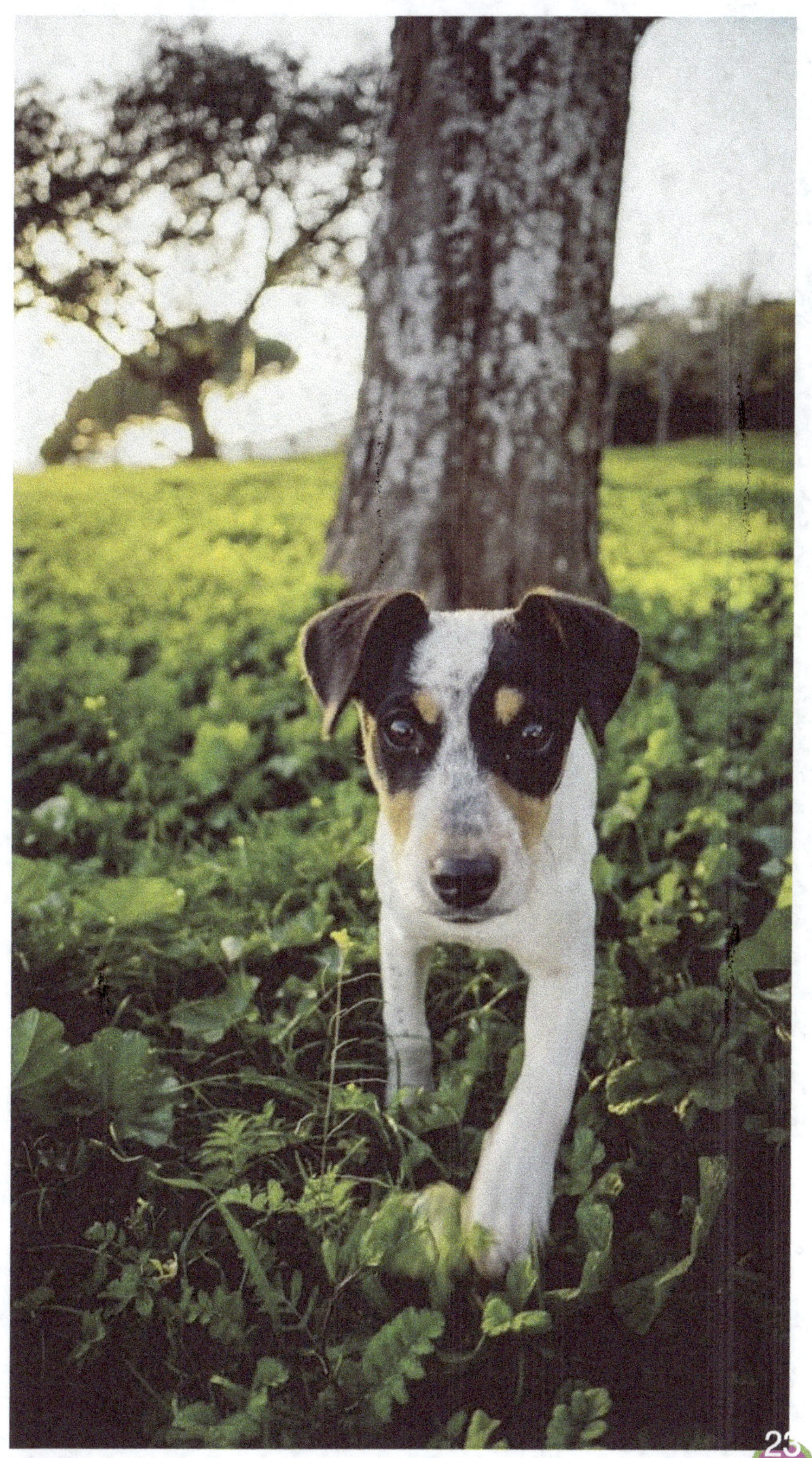

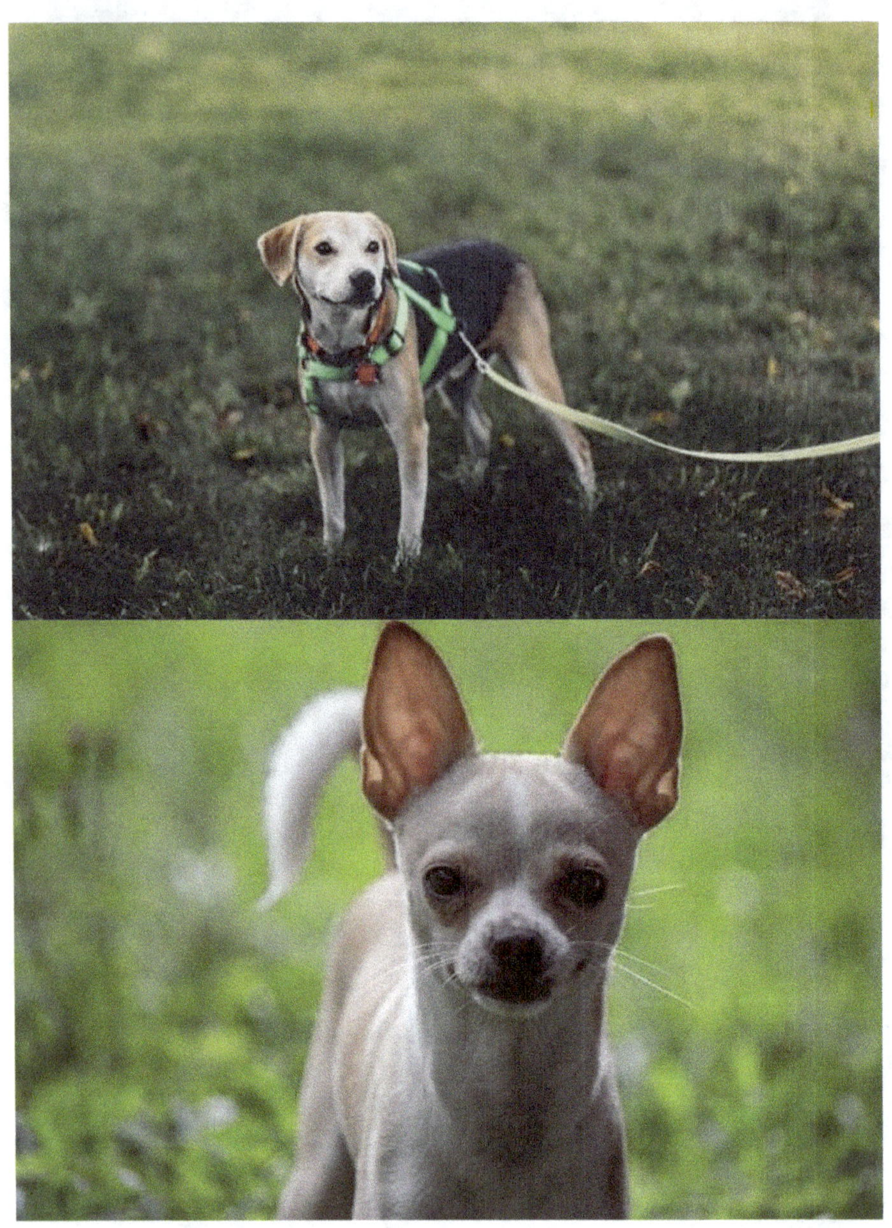

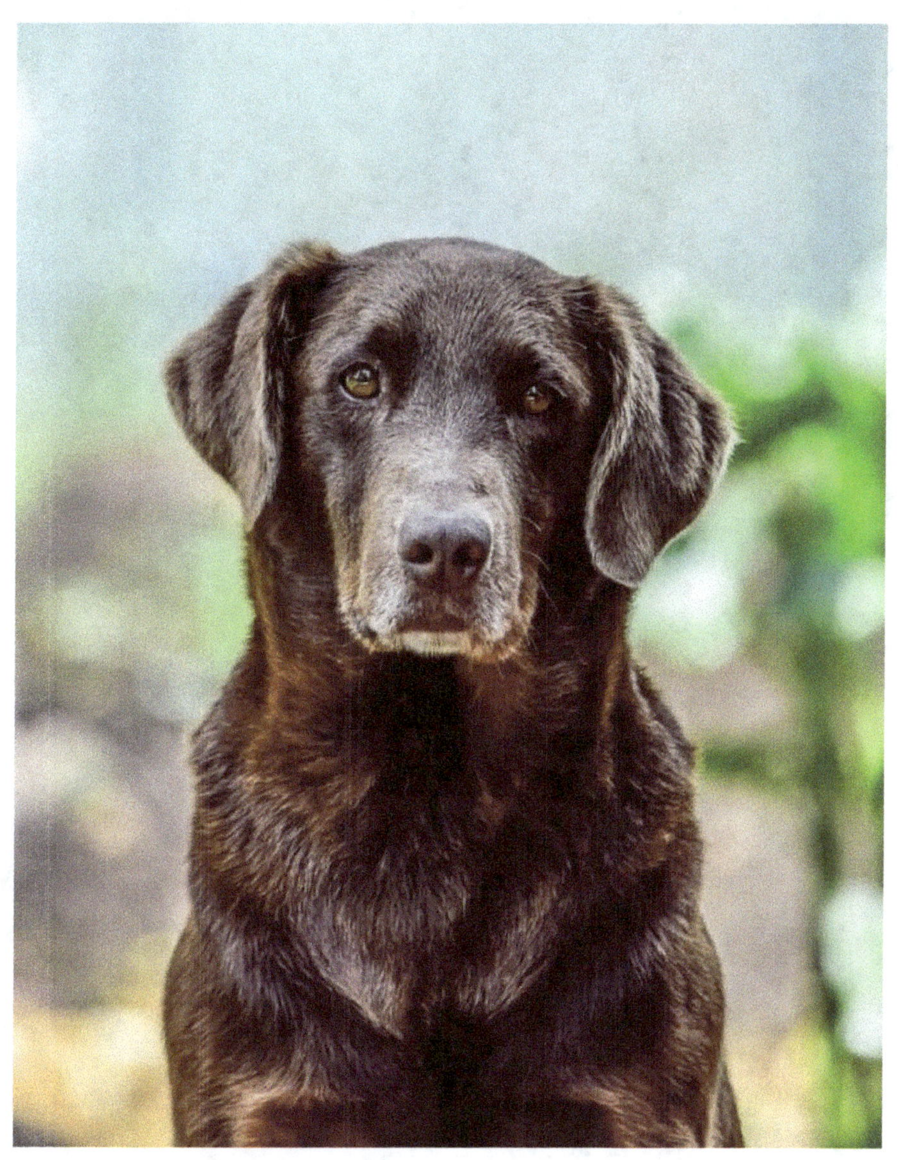

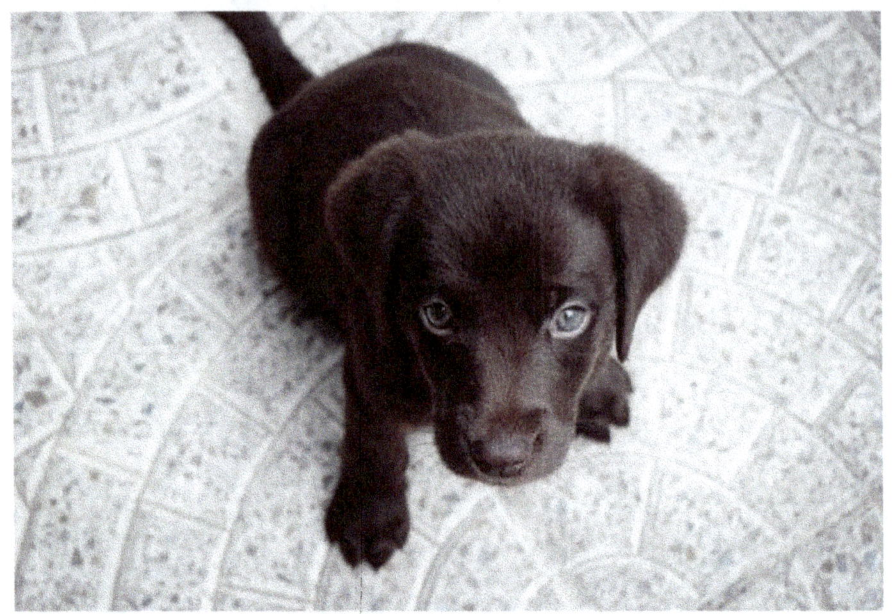

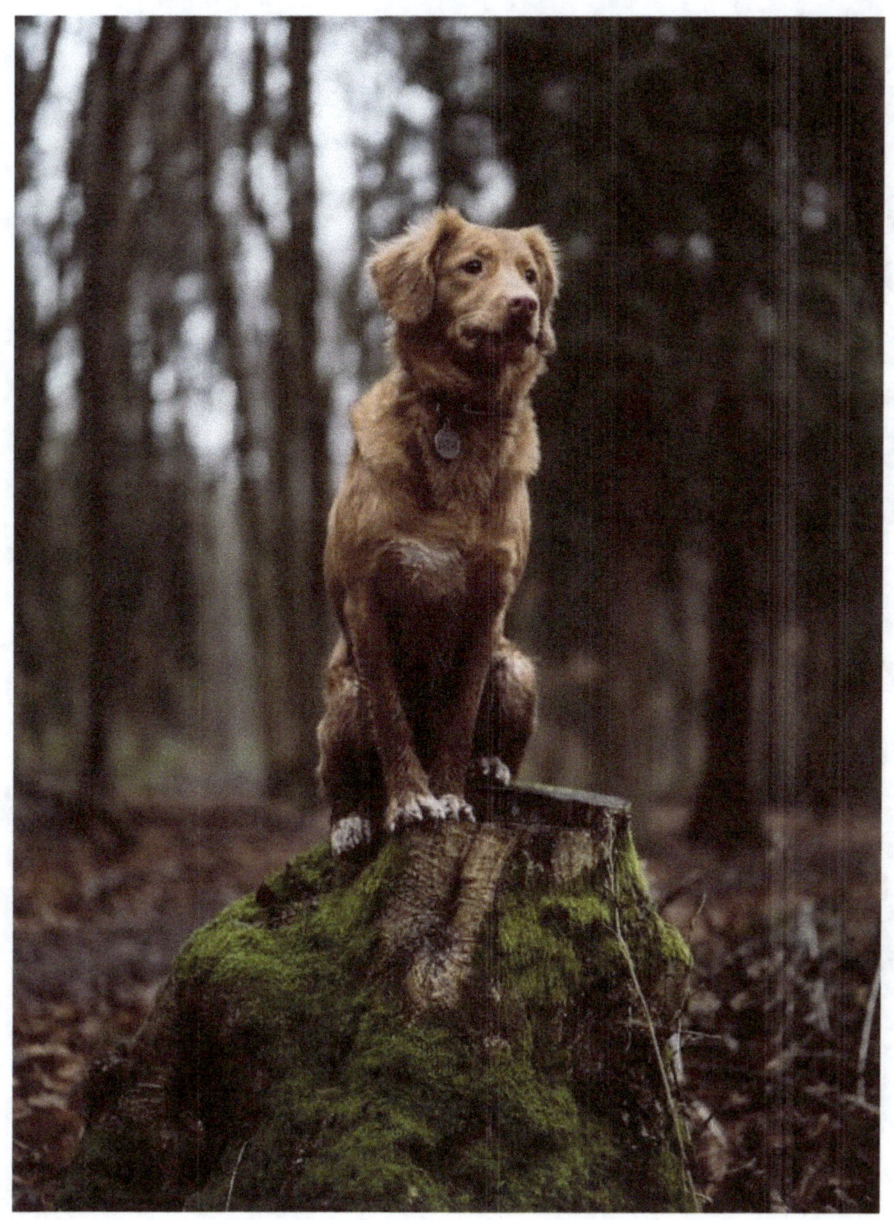

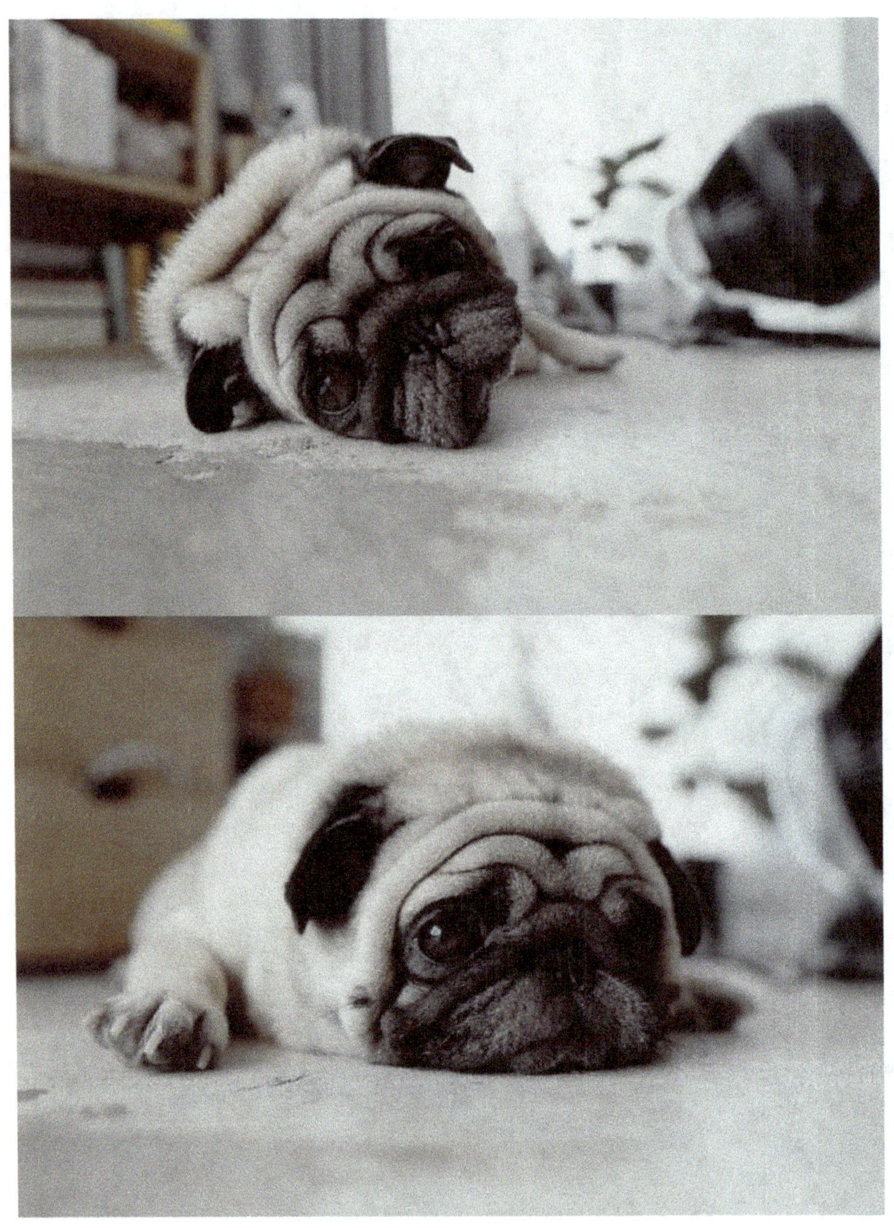

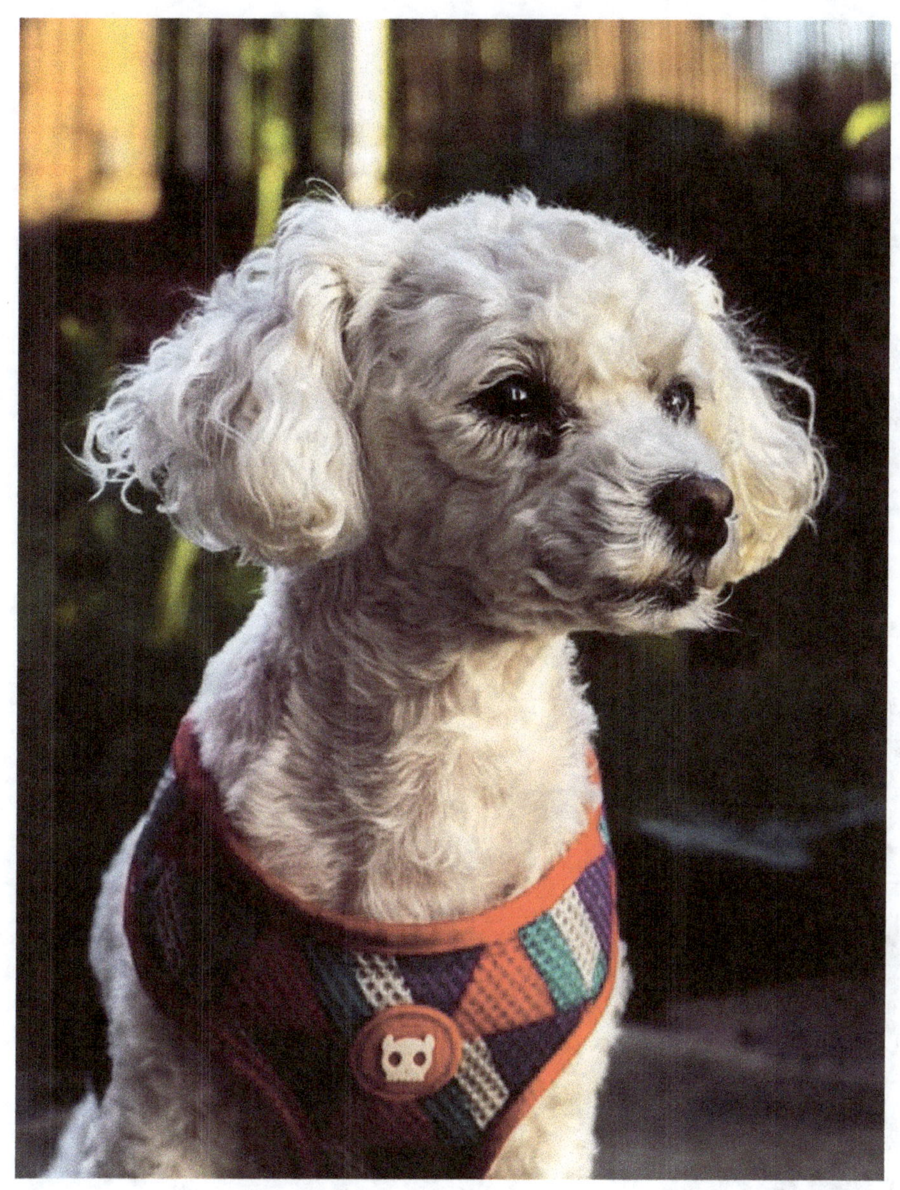

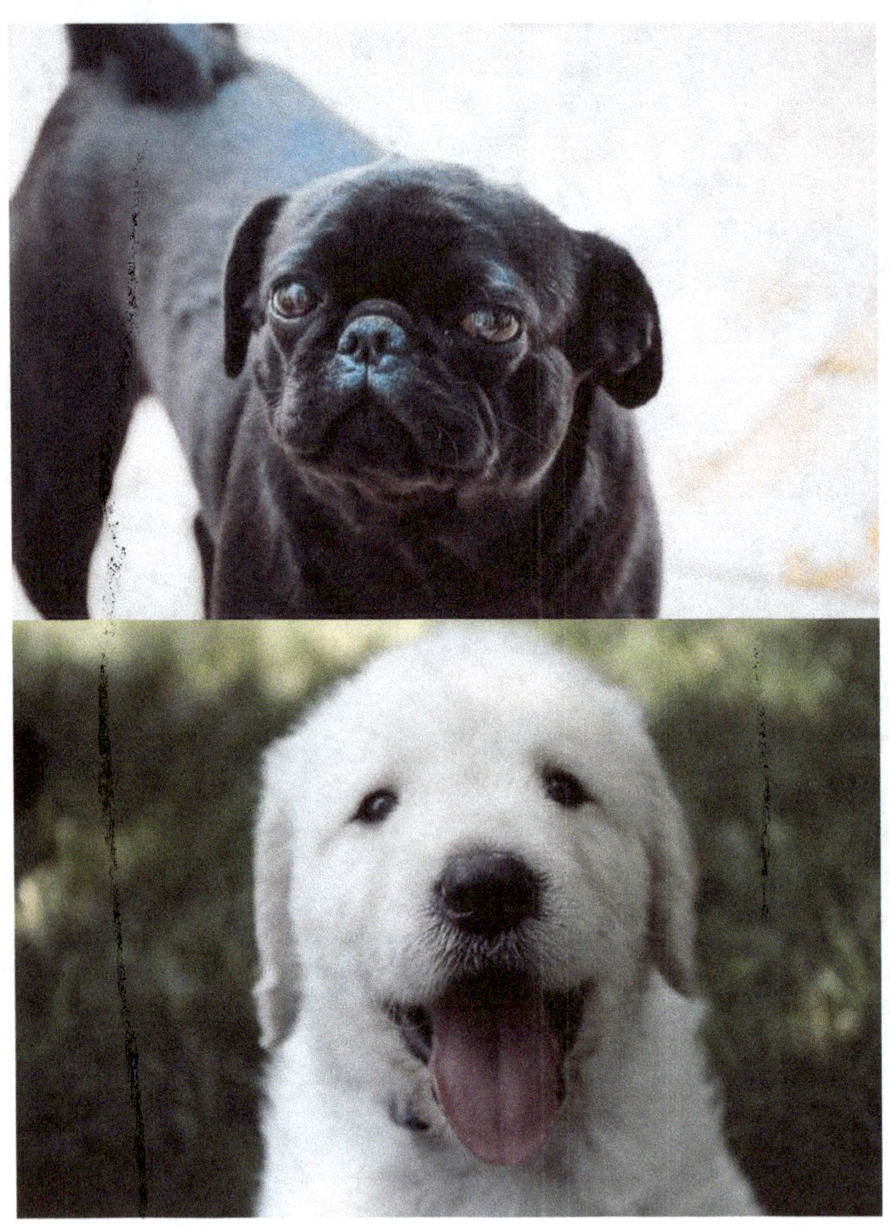

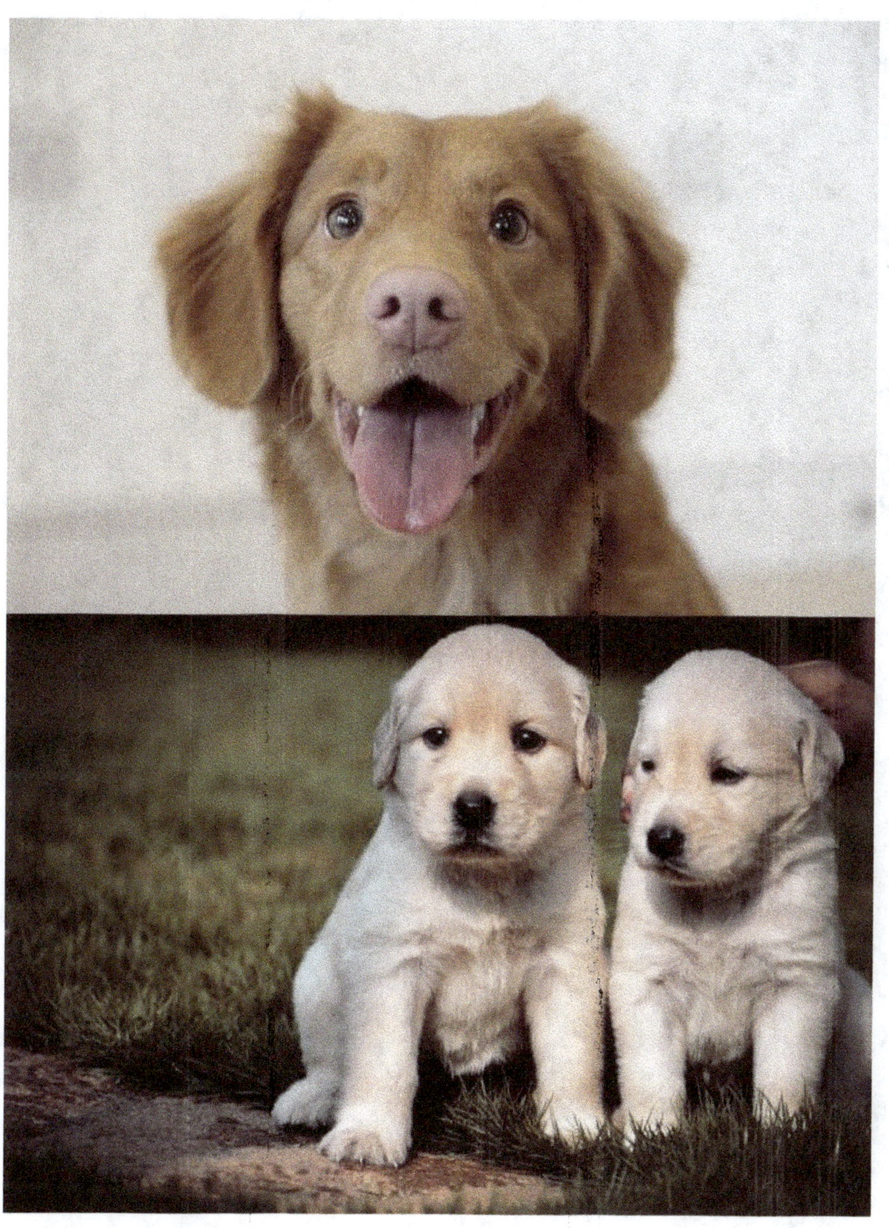

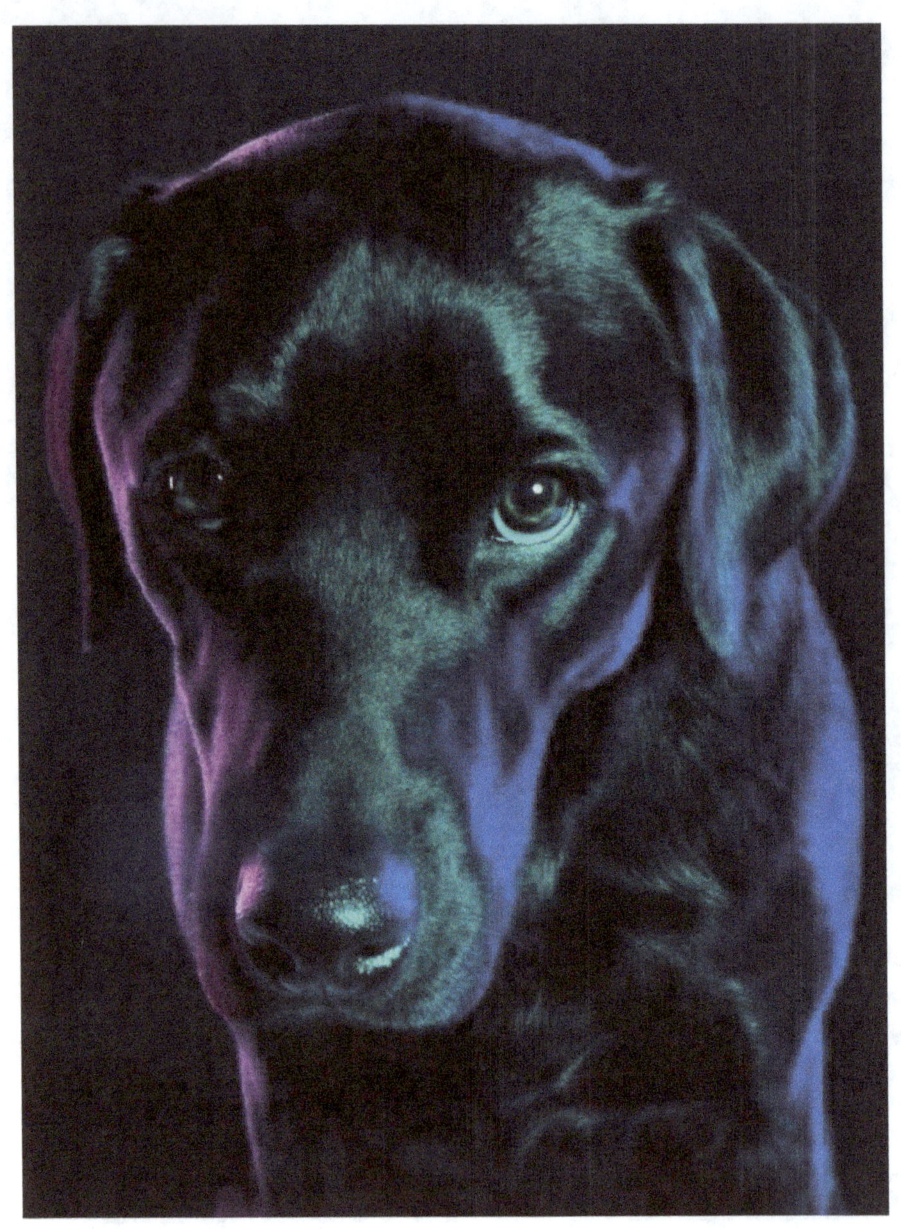

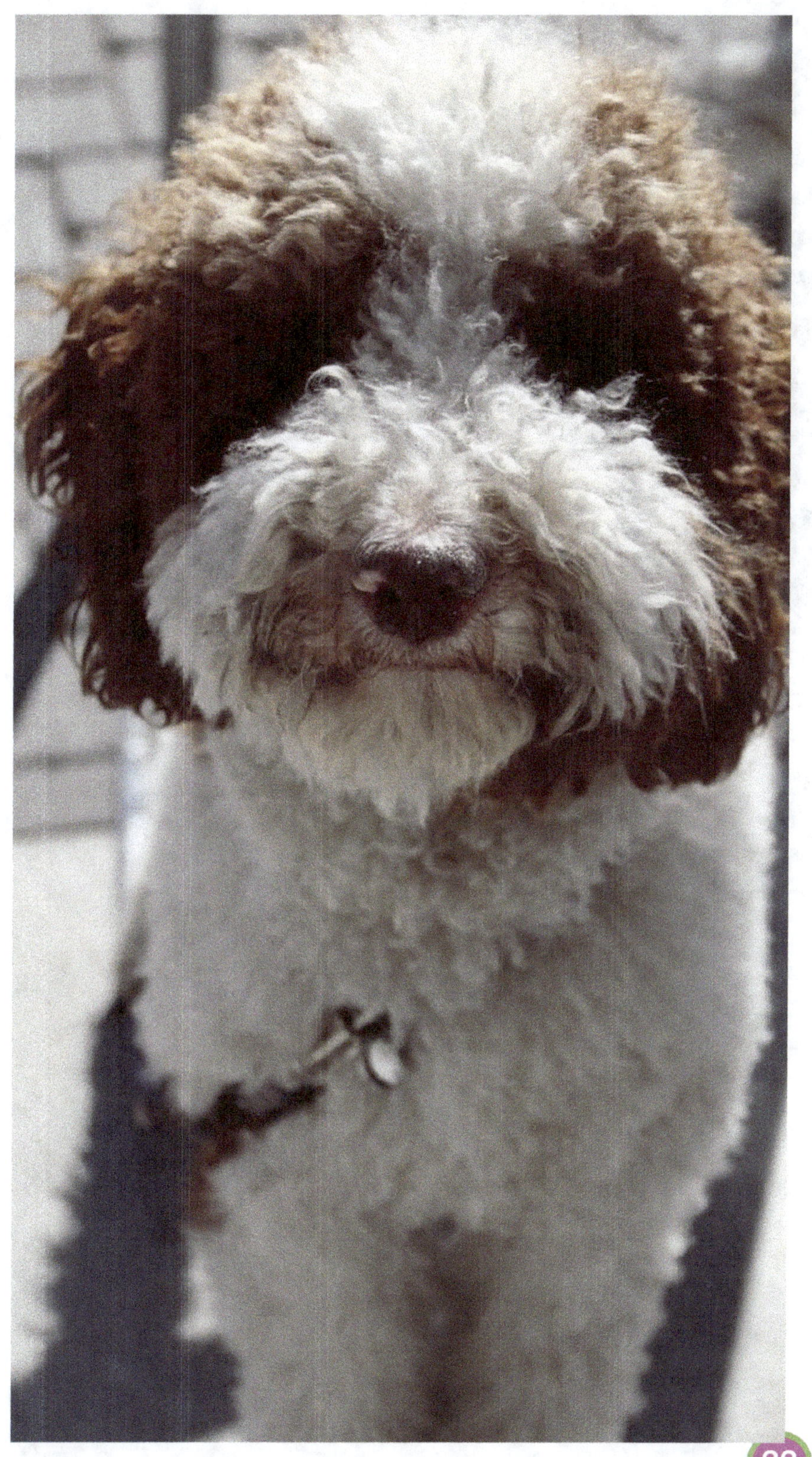

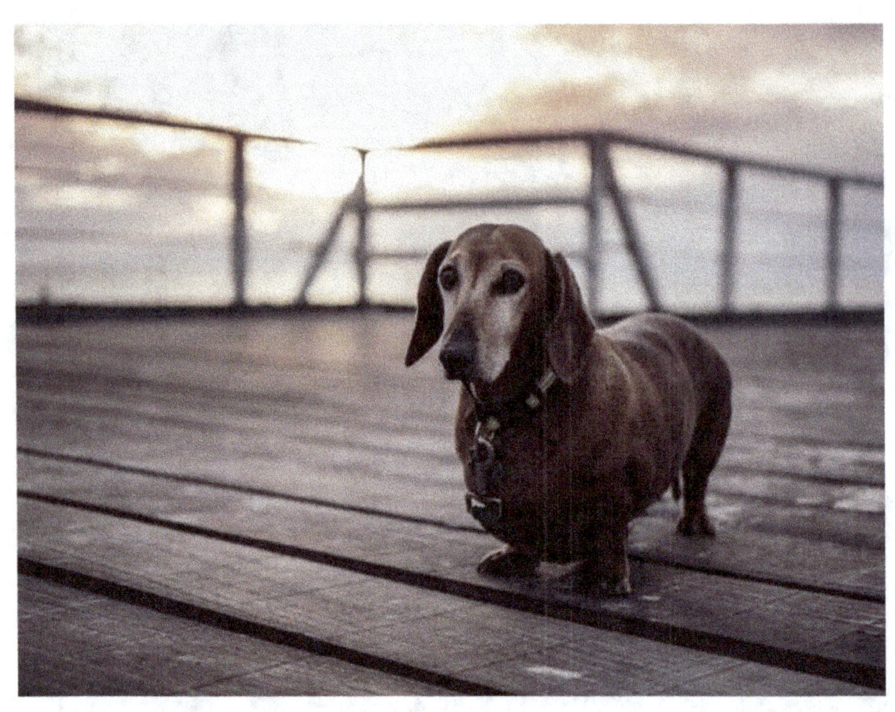

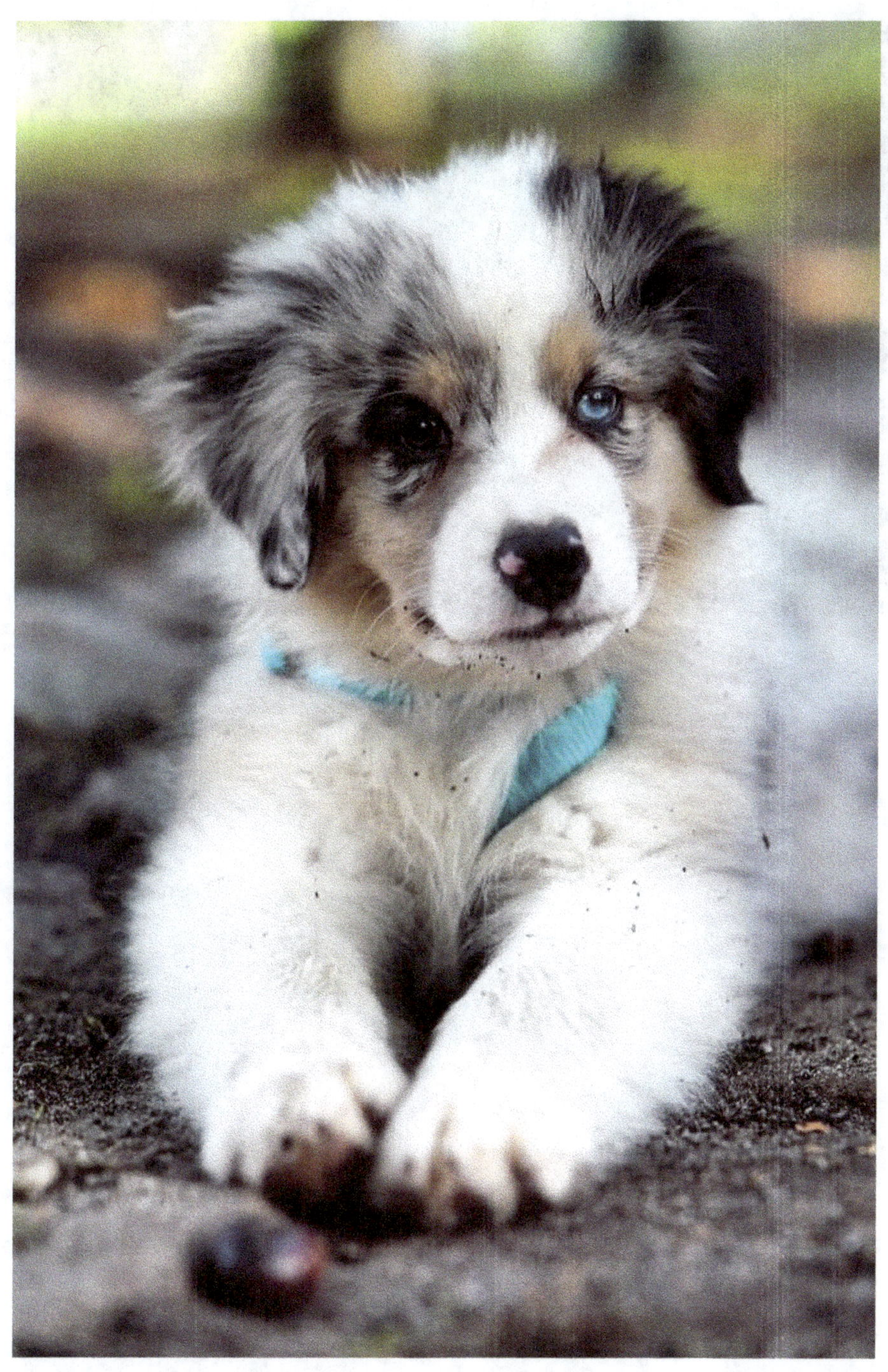

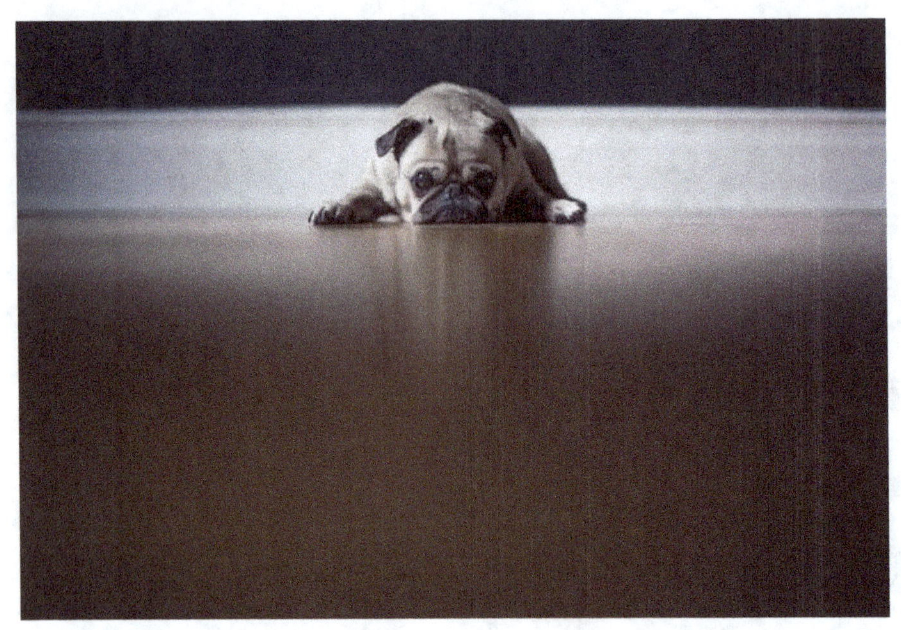

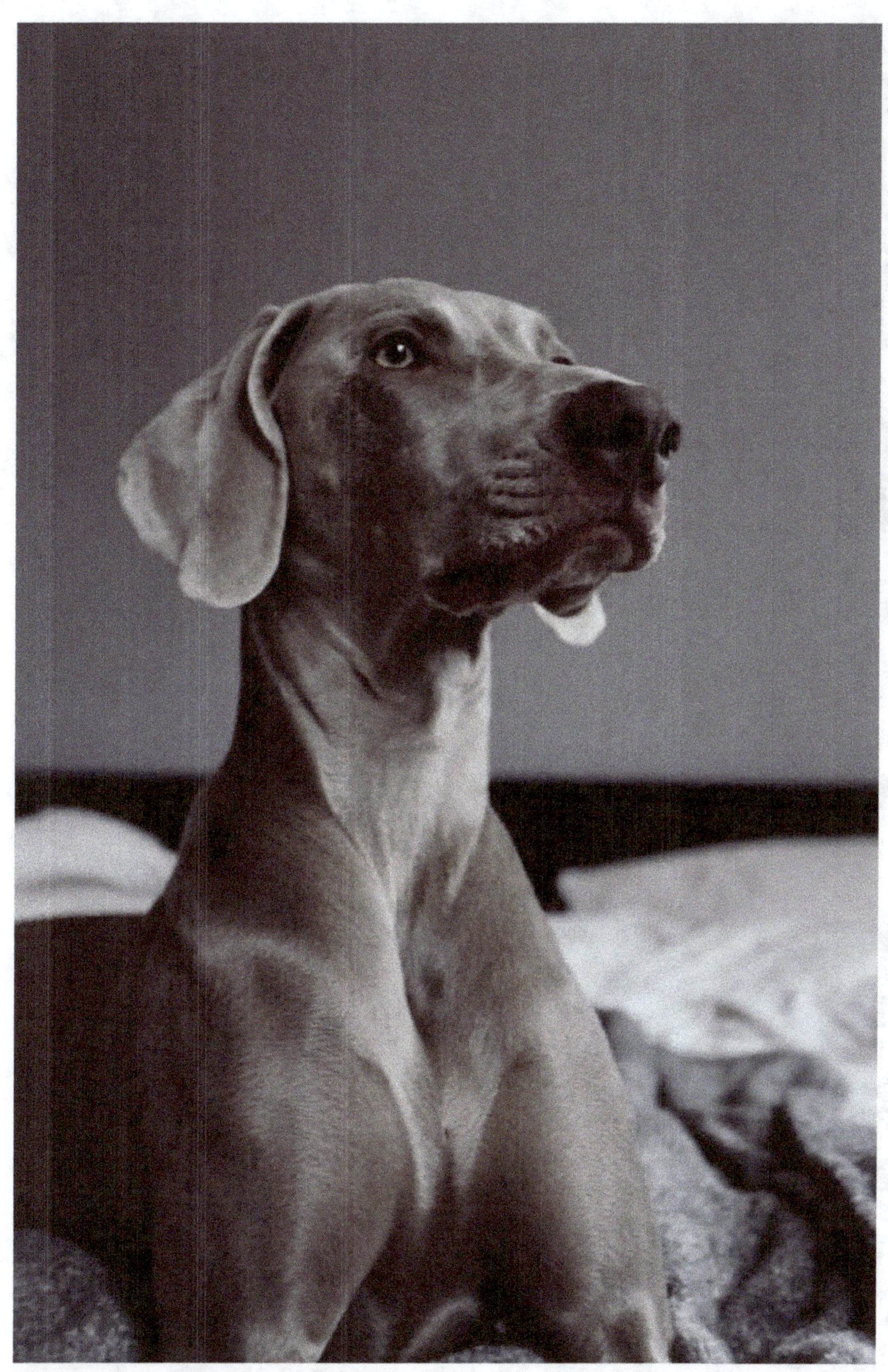

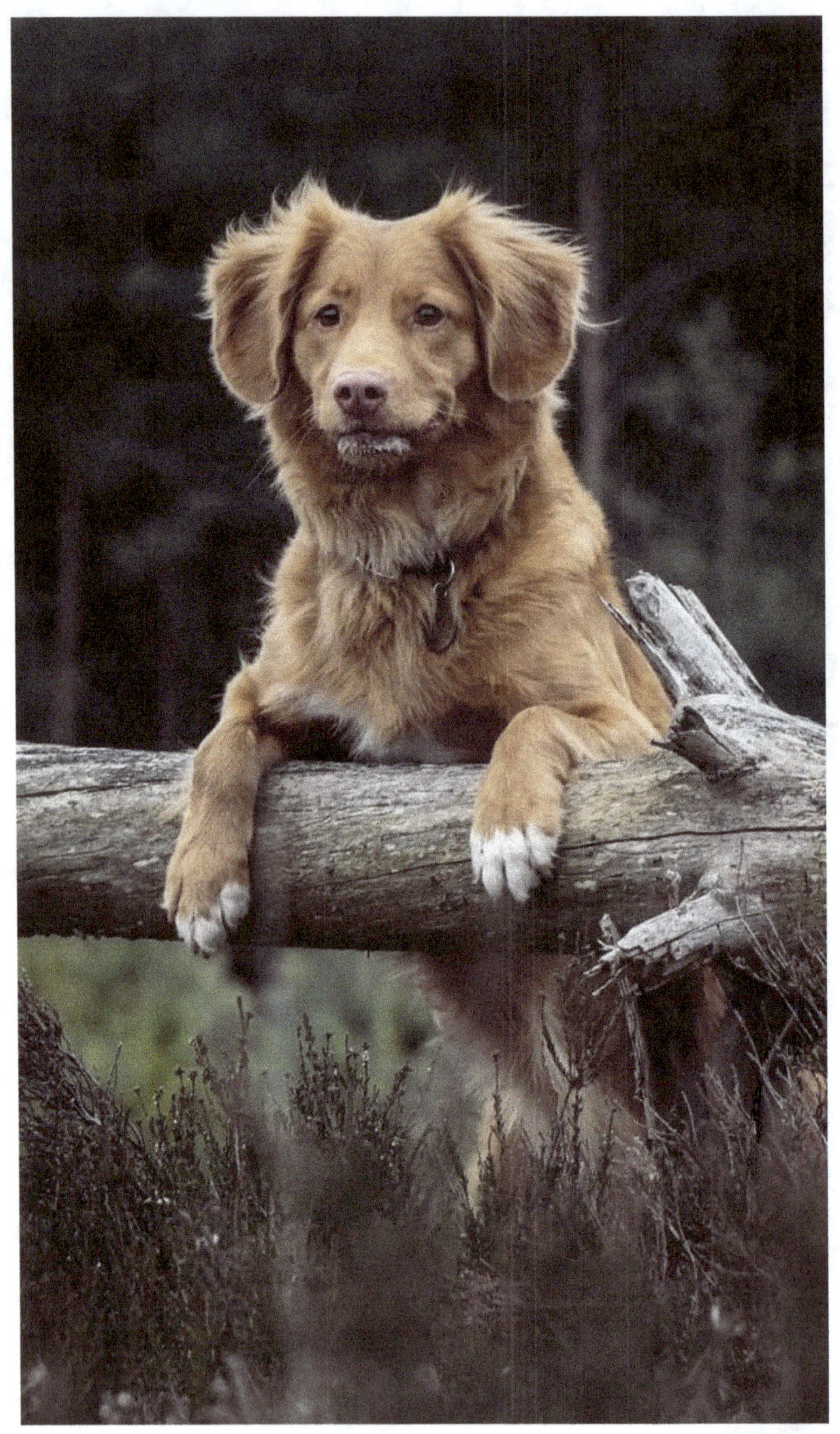

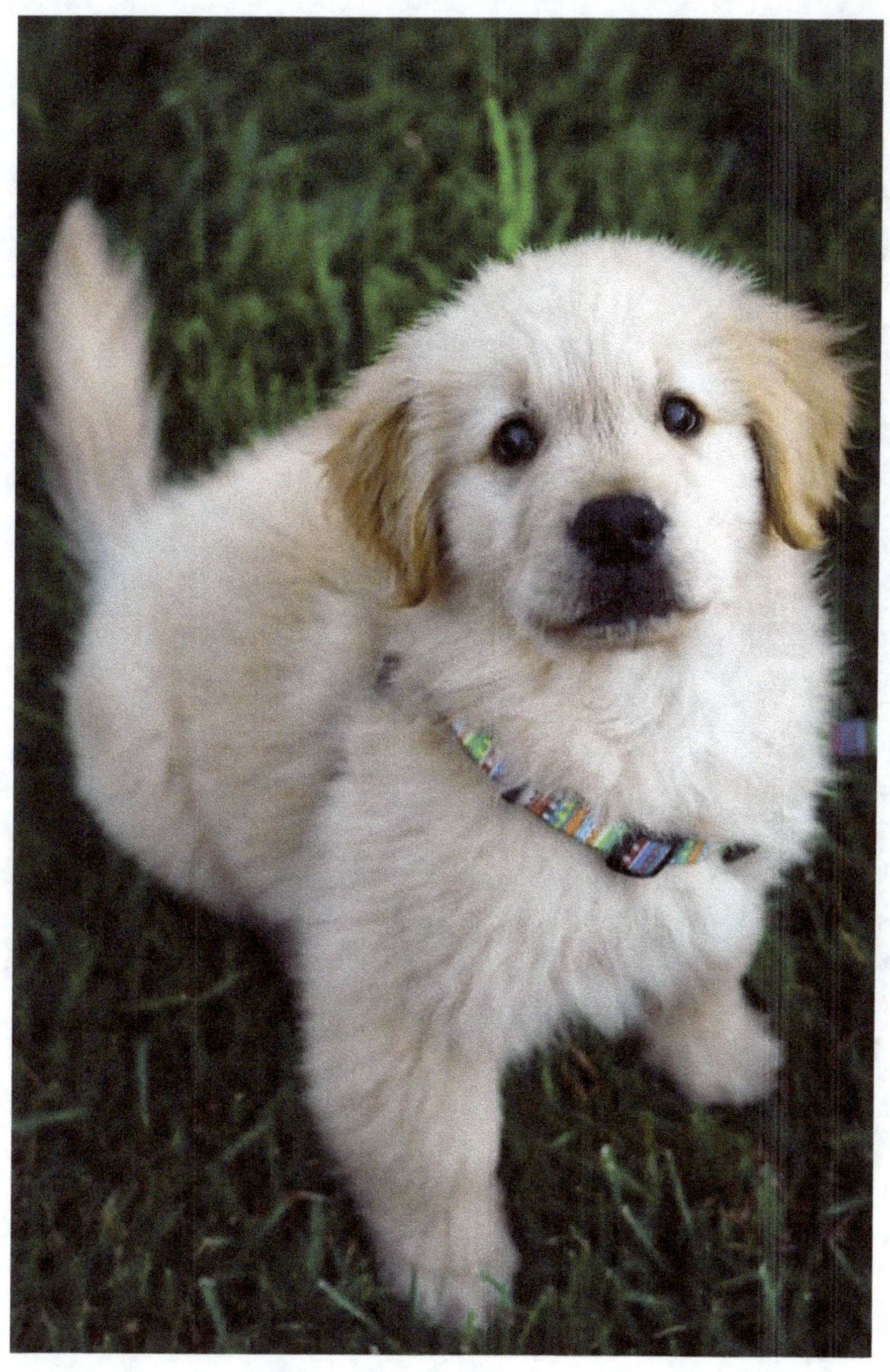

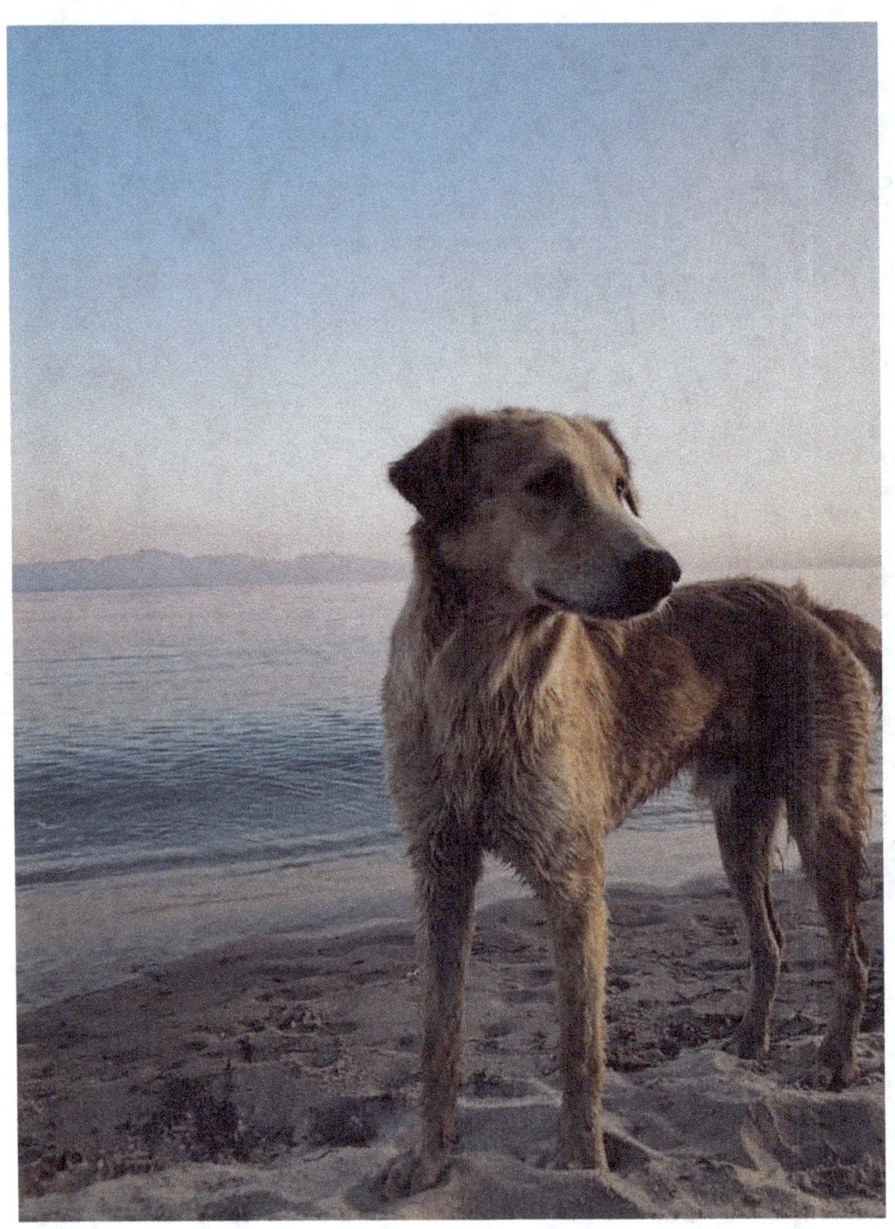

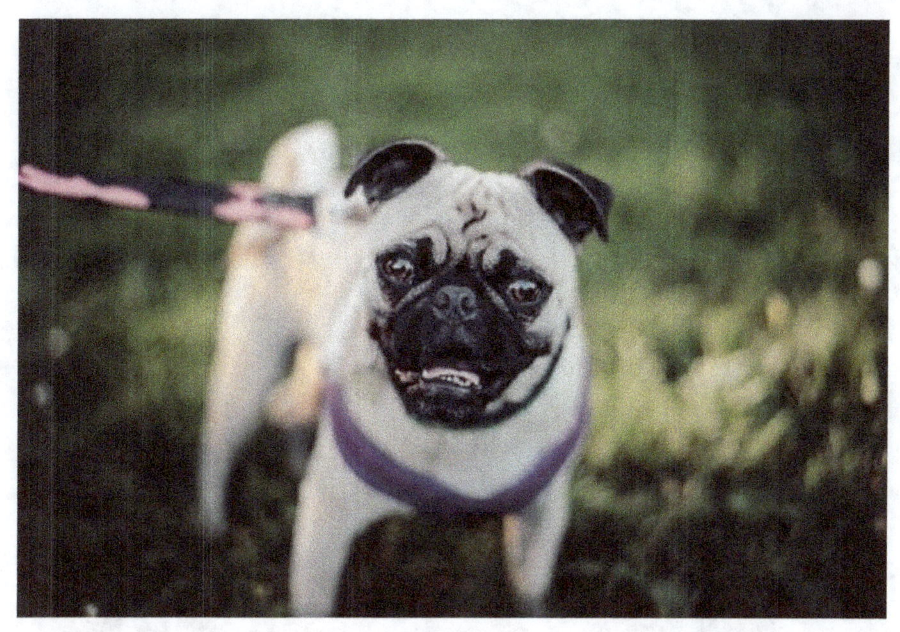

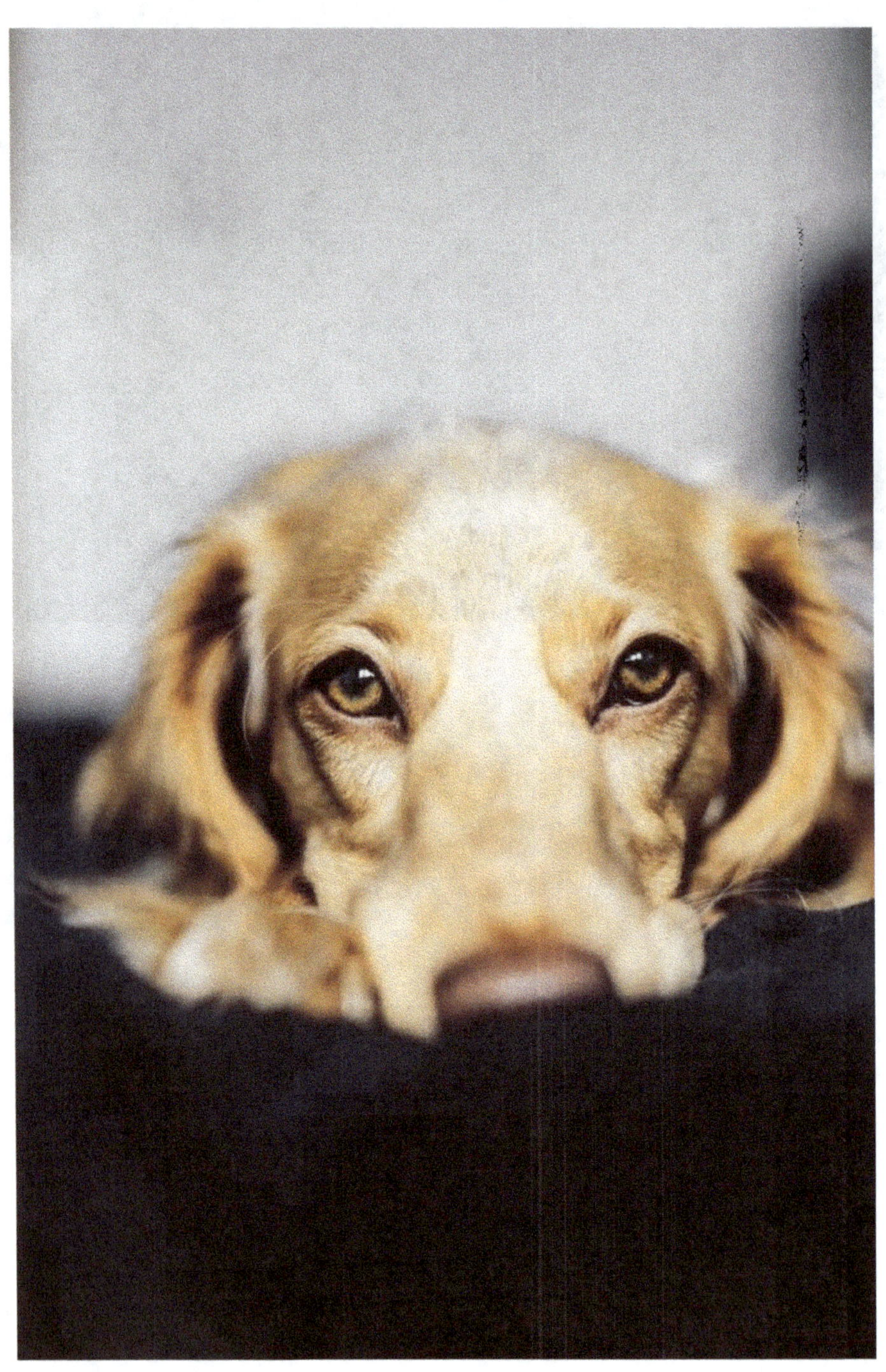

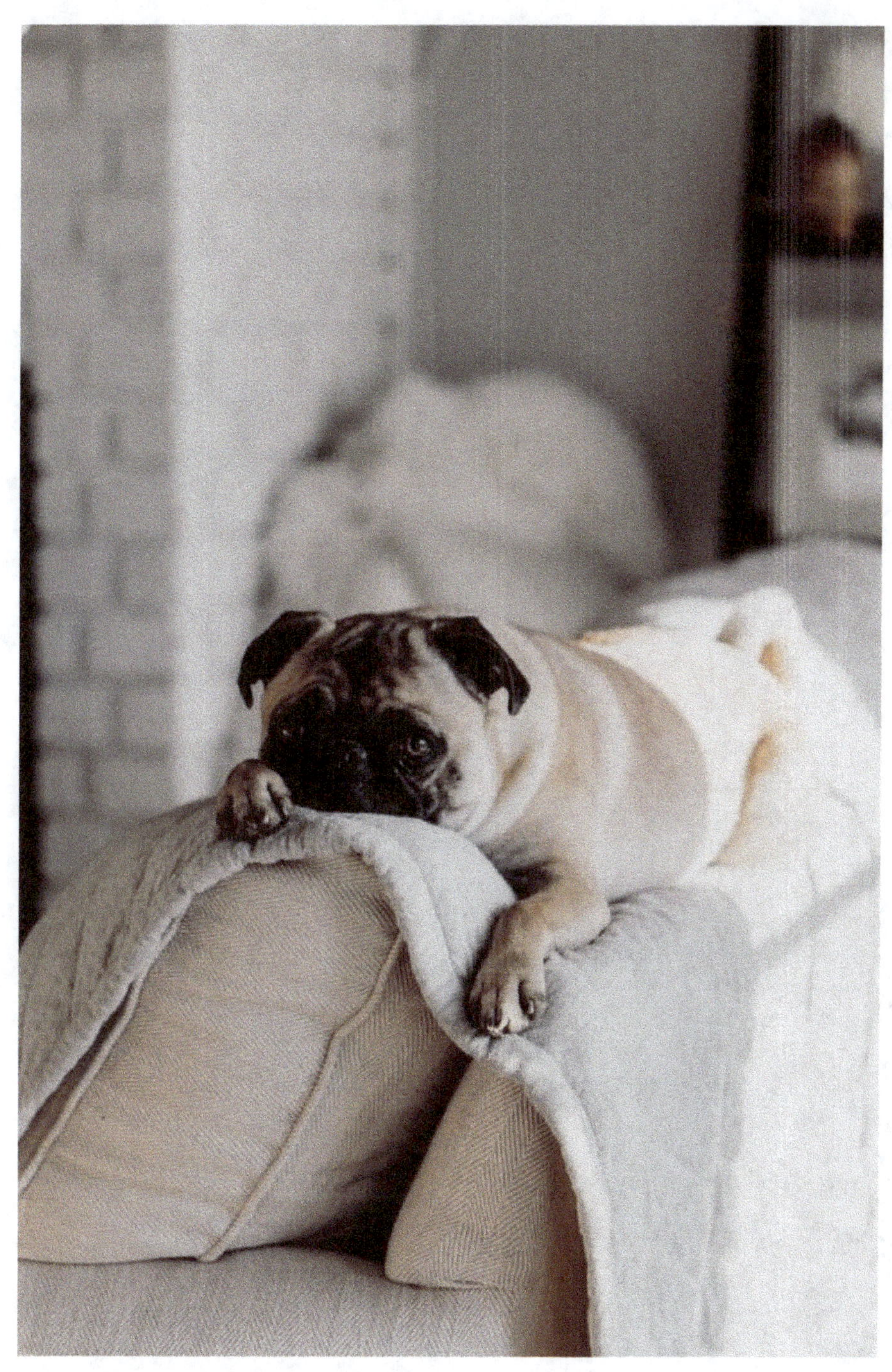

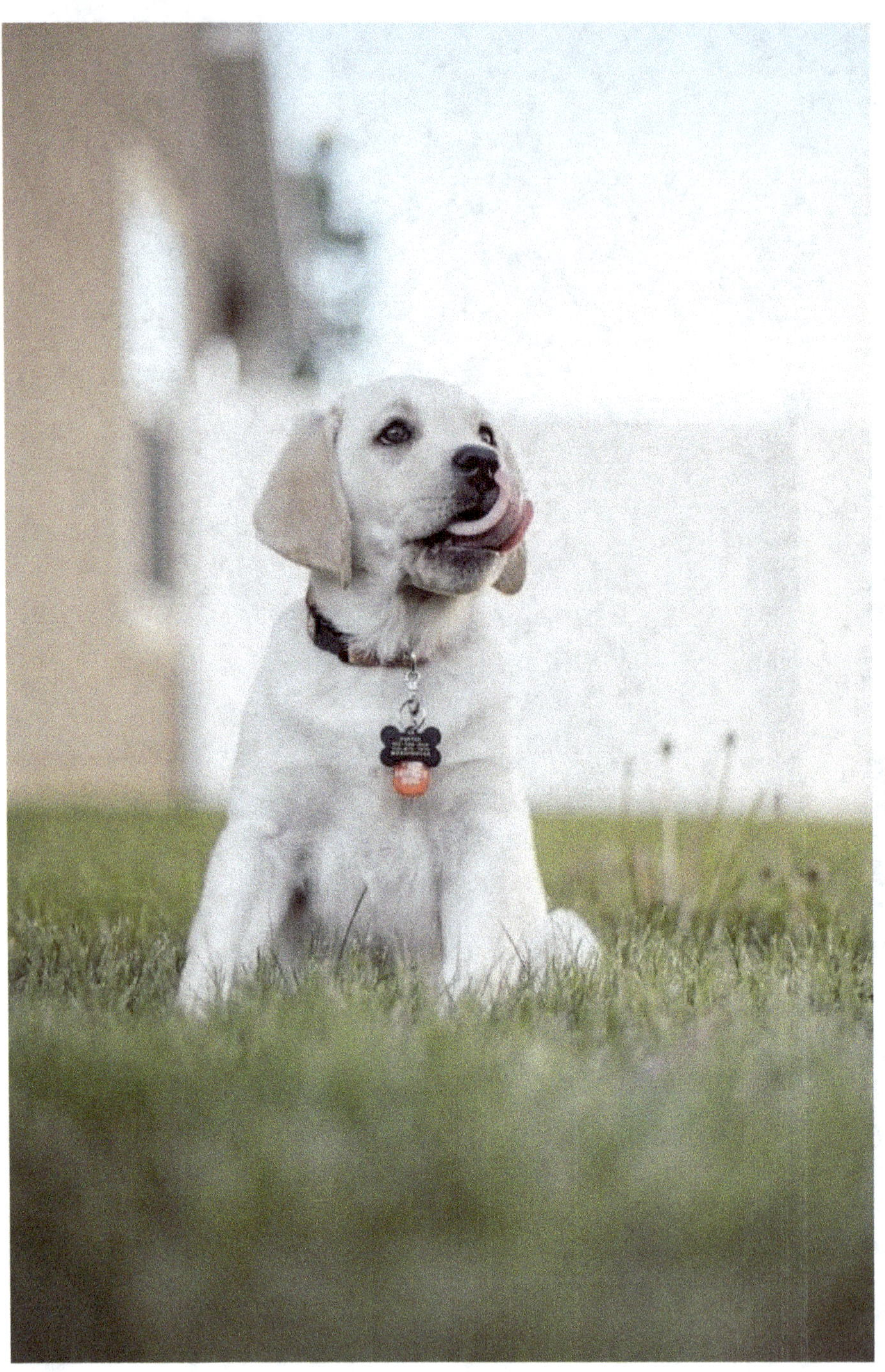

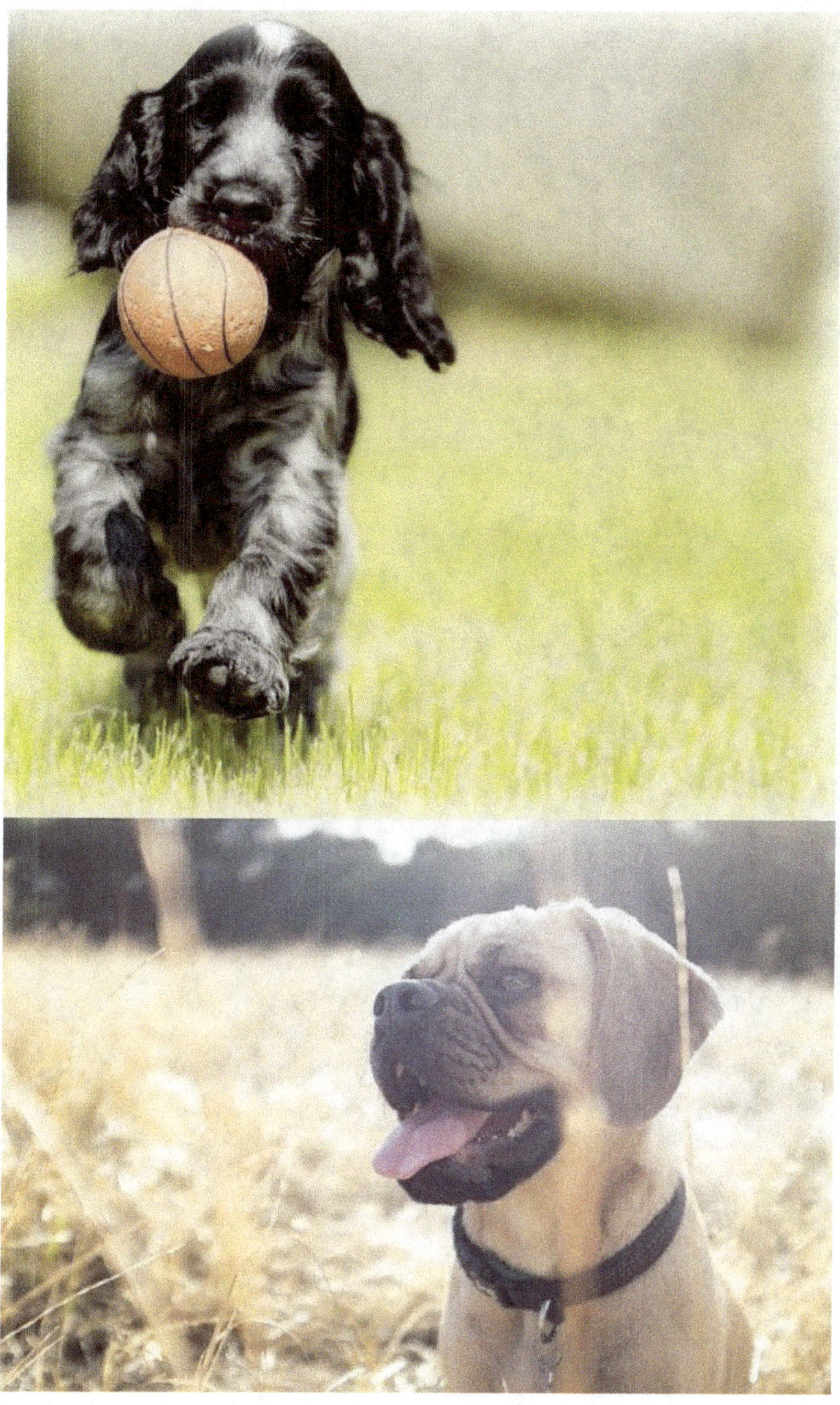

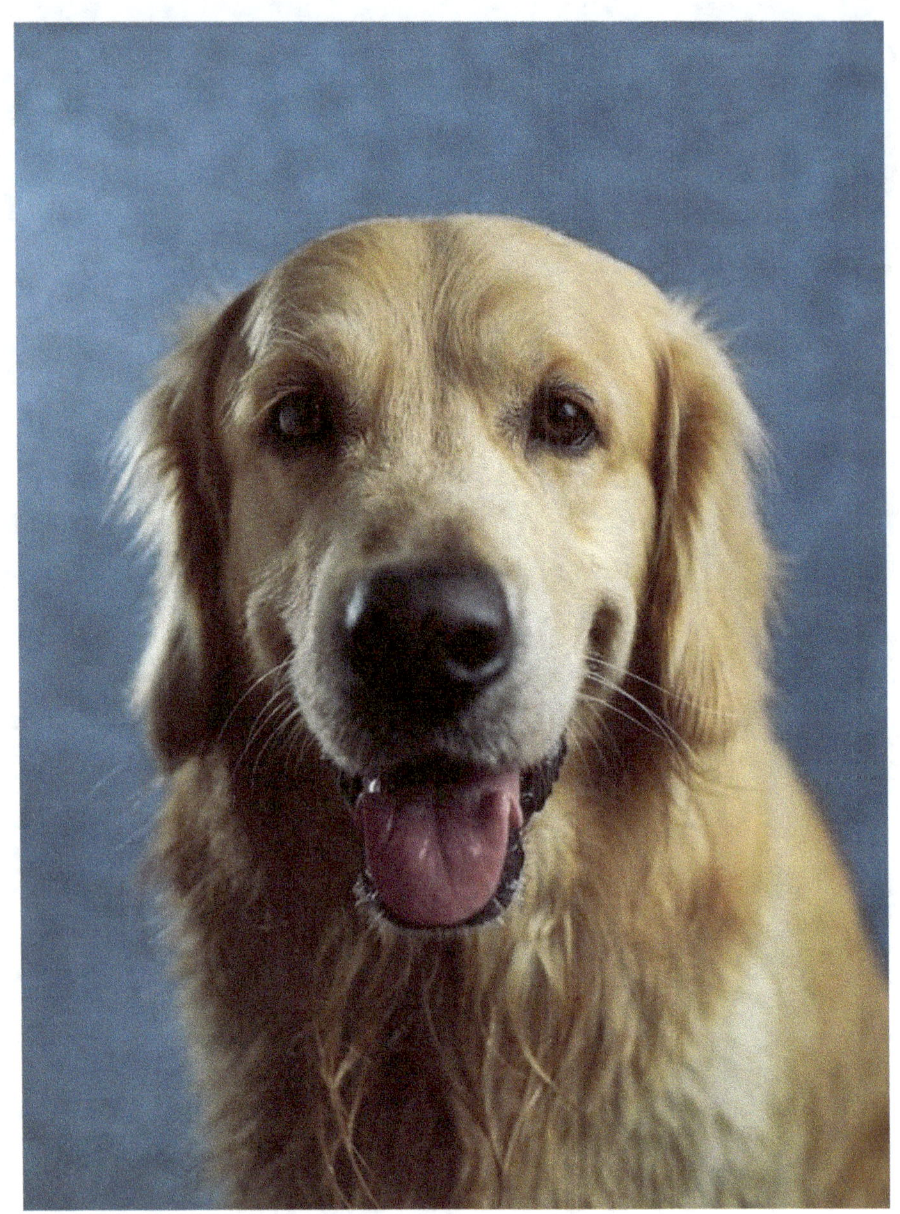

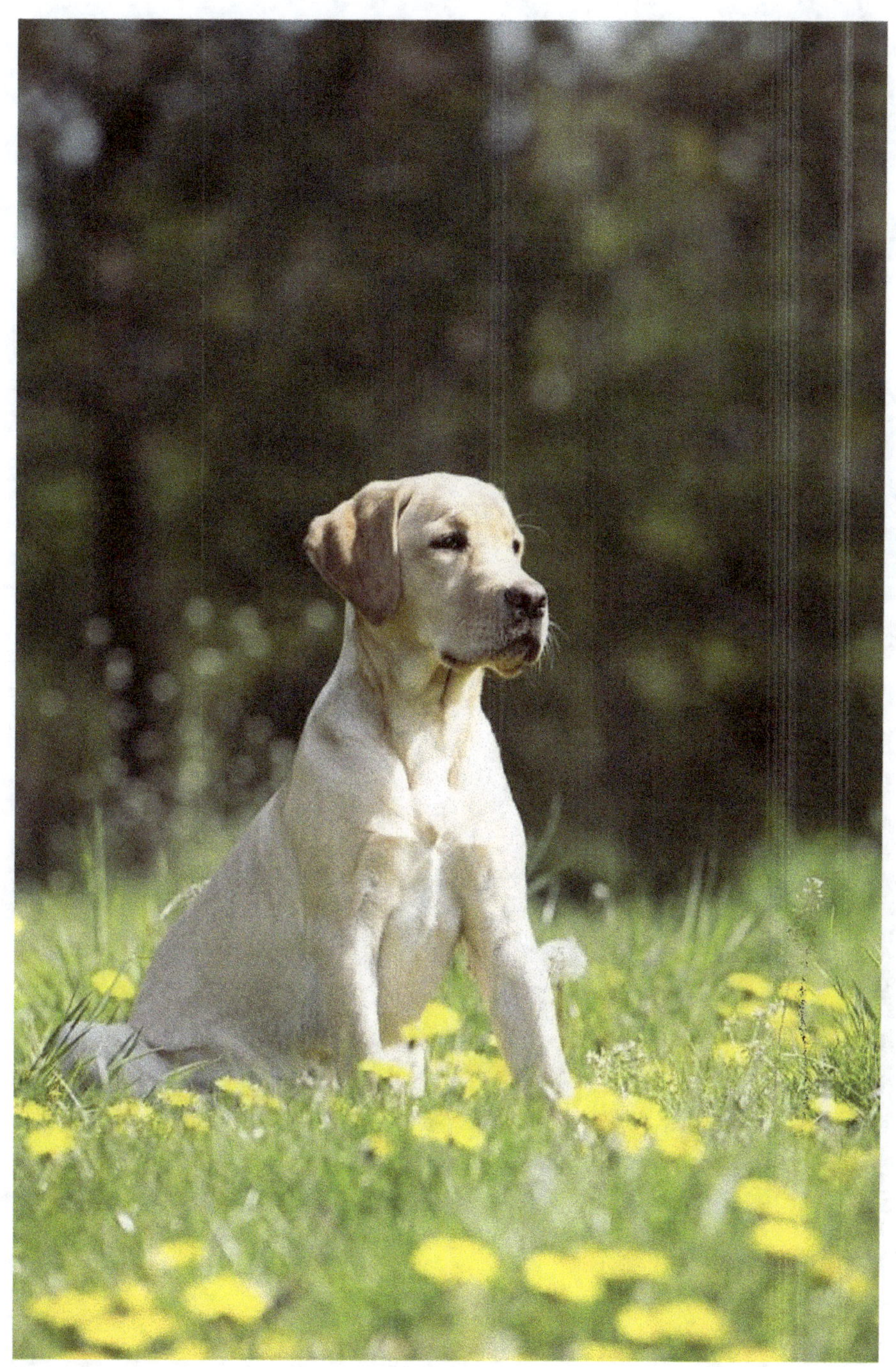

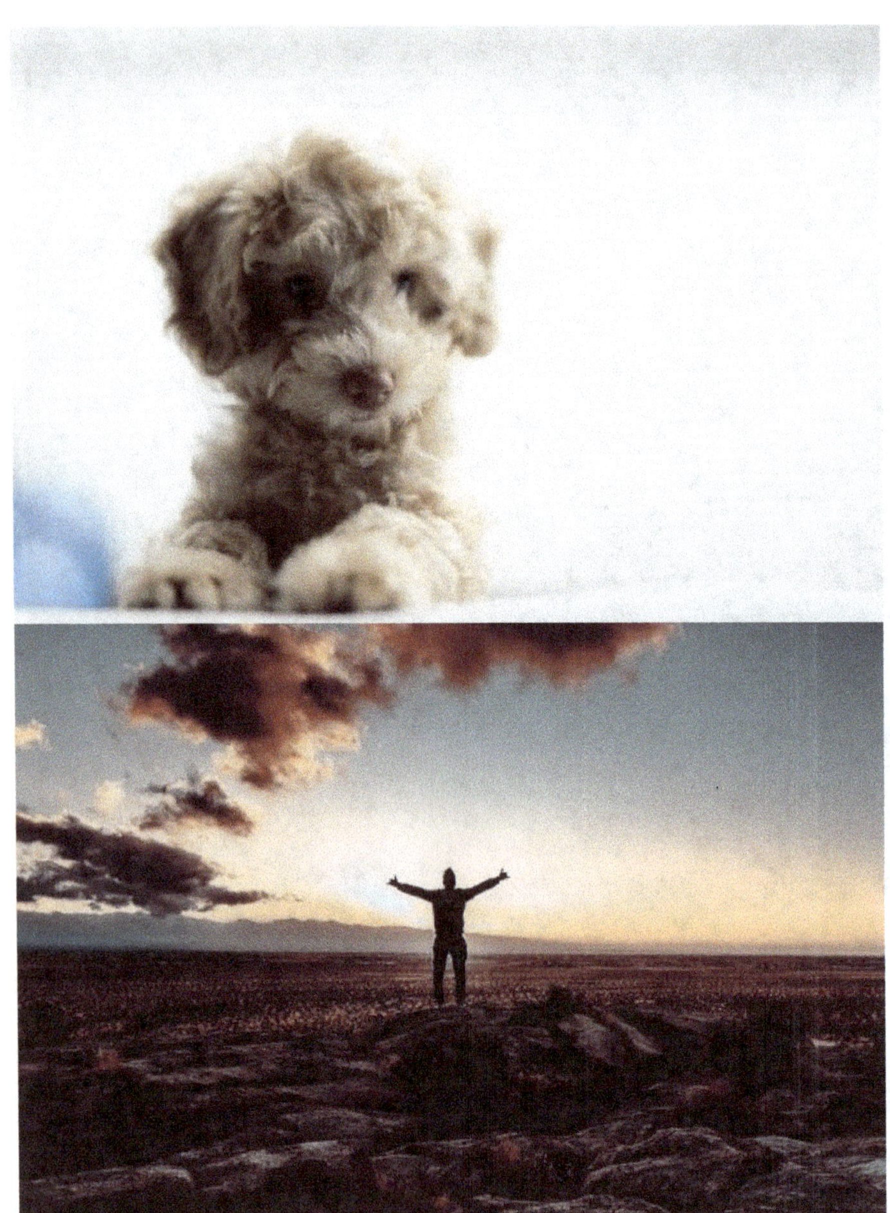

"In ancient times cats were worshipped asgods; they have not forgotten this." - TerryPratchett